The leader who shares
experience ensures a
bright future and leaves
a legacy of success.

Best Regards,
Juan Mora, VP Technology

degrees of
STRENGTH °

Also by the authors

Stomp the Elephant in the Office

Steven W. Vannoy & Craig W. Ross, 2008 Wister & Willows

Best Books Award Finalist, USA Book News

The 10 Greatest Gifts I Give My Children

Steven W. Vannoy, 1994 Simon & Schuster

degrees of
STRENGTH °

the innovative technique to
accelerate greatness

CRAIG W. ROSS & STEVEN W. VANNOY
Edited by Drew M. Ross

Wister
& Willows
Publishers Inc.

Wister & Willows, Publishers Inc.
10822 West Toller Drive, Suite 300
Littleton, CO 80127
www.verusglobal.com

Library of Congress Control Number 2011943035

Degrees of strength : the innovative technique to accelerate greatness / Craig W. Ross and Steven W. Vannoy.

ISBN 978-0-9793768-2-5
1. Leadership. I. Title
2011943035

Printed in Canada on acid-free paper.

"You are not here merely to make a living. You are here in order to enable the world to live more amply, with greater vision, with a finer spirit of hope and achievement. You are here to enrich the world. . . ."

-WOODROW WILSON
28th President of the United States

"Here's how."

- STEVEN W. VANNOY
Founder, Verus Global

Contents

BEFORE IT BEGINS...viii

CHAPTER ONE
Rachel: The Quest for Responsibility...1
The single greatest issue in leadership
The acceleration moment

CHAPTER TWO
Case Study: Changing the Approach to Change.. 13
Who Accelerators are
The compelling fact that is true about the people around you

CHAPTER THREE
Roberto: The Degrees of Strength Move from Red to Green 19
The Degrees of Strength *technique*
The 3 Mind Factors

CHAPTER FOUR
Case Study: Execution and Excellence – Even in Tough Situations 37
Questions Trigger the Mind
Forward Focus Questions

CHAPTER FIVE
Andrea: A Leader Gets Over Herself.. 43
Why are people so stupid? . . . Playing the perfection game
The language for Degrees of Strength

CHAPTER SIX
Case Study: The Generator of Trust... 67
Accelerators are trust generators
Five steps of a trust-based partnership approach

CHAPTER SEVEN

Eric and Luc: Transforming Performance.. 71
Leaders are corrupt . . . and the Degrees of Strength *experiment*
Addressing poor performance

CHAPTER EIGHT

Case Study: Agility, Agility, Agility 89
Agility is a skill . . . and responsibility is a choice
Going from worst to first

CHAPTER NINE

Rachel: What Leadership Can Be About.. 95
How to make servant leadership work (when you don't like the person)
Voting team members off the island

CHAPTER TEN

The Five Choices Accelerators Make 107
What is your team talking about?
Suddenly, you can deliver anything – sooner and more often

EPILOGUE: Moving Forward is Never Over 111
Who am I to rationalize my poor behavior?
The most important leadership work you'll do

WITH GRATITUDE.. 118

APPENDICES 121
3 Mind Factors
Recipe for Partnership
Trust-Based Partnerships Framework
Five Choices Accelerators Make

Before It Begins

How effective are you at getting the best from others? (From yourself?) Do you believe your team possesses a potential that, if realized, would transform how it performs – and enrich team members' lives in the process?

The inspired story and real-life case studies that follow are for those who know that within each person, every team, family, and organization, there is a potential so considerable that, once achieved, alters and heightens the course forward. Within these pages is the technique necessary to accelerate one's ability to deliver that greatness.

It's worth asking your team: How many people in our organization have the skill to bring forth from you a greater understanding and effort – so much so that you know you are delivering on your potential? (You probably don't need a national poll to tell you the percentage of people who are doing this is small.) Equally important to ask your colleagues: What would this team achieve if we were more capable at leading this way?

Those who are most skillful at ensuring a vision becomes a reality know that everyone is capable of doing extraordinary acts. And, of this group, the most exceptional are developing this skill in others in every interaction of every day. The Degrees of Strength technique is how they do it. It's what your team can do to accelerate performance immediately.

Two decades of working with teams on six continents has made this clear: When you apply the Degrees of Strength technique, you differentiate yourself as a leader. Those who have mastered this skill will tell you that the technique of Degrees of Strength is uniquely different than the traditional approach to strengths-based living and leading: It's a paradigm shift, a discipline in focus, and an action forward . . . that makes anything possible.

It all starts with this question: What difference would it make if your team – or your family – had no weaknesses? Seriously – no joke: How would you lead if every strength and quality you needed for those around you to perform at higher levels already existed within them?

CHAPTER ONE

Rachel: The Quest for Responsibility

"We don't have a chance.

"Honestly, that's what I thought when I arrived," Rachel recalled. "You'd expect different behavior from leaders within a company this size. But if there's one thing I've discovered over the years . . ." She stopped. "Can we be frank here?"

"Please do," I said.

"The single greatest issue in leadership is so few people take responsibility. If you can't get a team to speak up, act, and be accountable, you're not going to win," Rachel said. "Sure, when you get to this level, people are professional and have skills. But honestly, I'm often shocked at how irresponsible people can be."

"It's one of those key issues we hear about in our sessions with organizations around the world," I said.

Rachel nodded at me. "If I've been successful at anything since I met you, it's supporting people in their move from halfhearted efforts to taking initiative, saying what needs to be said, and taking action. That organizational mindset and capability shift changes everything."

I recognized this and asked, "We hear different definitions of this. What do you mean, *halfhearted*?" (She looked at me with a face that said, "Really?")

"By halfhearted I mean they're not 'all in.' It means they're not delivering their true potential. It means they're waiting for someone else to do or say something before they take responsibility. And it manifests itself in countless ways. For example, everyone wants the organization to succeed, but too often that is translated to 'only if I succeed first.' They talk 'one team,' but then they don't share their resources because they fear their department will be vulnerable and not look good.

"Or, I used to see this: Success doesn't mean the team wins – it means achieving your department or career objectives. When that's the definition of success, it results in few people willing to make the tough decision that's necessary for everyone to win. Because making that choice means standing up, addressing the real and sometimes ugly facts about where we are right now, and leading us in an improved direction – even if that direction means giving up a piece of your pie. And this requires people to be vulnerable."

I nodded and leaned forward. "There's that word: *vulnerable*. It can be complicated. We hear leaders stating that it's a necessary quality for growth – and yet other people distance themselves from the idea."

"It's certainly a double-edged word," Rachel said. "There's no way we want our team thinking we will leave ourselves exposed to flaws or liabilities. On the other hand, we need people to be humble, to admit they're not perfect. Not for the sake of focusing on or allowing ourselves to be inadequate, but for the purpose of being able to take accountability."

"As you've developed that ability in your team, what has it looked like in action?" I asked.

Rachel thought for a moment, then said, "In our meeting yesterday, Luc – you'll get to meet him later – he interrupted me and said, 'Rachel, before we deploy, I think we should run one more round of tests. I'm not confident we received accurate data with the earlier series.' And then he added, 'I apologize. And I promise we'll improve the testing.'"

"It takes skill to seize a remarkable leadership opportunity that's presented in such a way," I said.

"Count me as one who used to be blind to such moments! Luc's team is responsible for making sure the tests are accurate. In the past, I would have vented my frustration with him – another round of testing would delay our ability to hit target." She laughed slightly, "But there he was, being vulnerable and providing full information, which ultimately would set us up for greater success. To seize the moment, I had to see the strength in his action and the situation and leverage it so we'd create greater accountability moving forward."

As I expected, Rachel was thinking about and performing in her role as divisional president differently from when I saw her last. As is done with all the leaders who've been immersed in the Degrees of Strength technique, I was returning months later to support her team's integration and sustainability of the skill. Given what she'd just shared about how she addressed Luc's performance, I made a note to myself: Later, as I spent time with other members of her team, I would be curious to see if those around her interpreted her changed leadership approach as soft. Would they think that Rachel was letting Luc off the hook? Would she be perceived as not ensuring people were accountable?

Rachel seemed to read my mind. "Accountability is an individual choice. You're not going to get far mandating it," she said. "And it's my job as the leader to improve Luc's ability to make greater choices, as well as create the environment that encourages those choices."

"That's terrific awareness, Rachel," I said. "It's indicative of a paradigm from which we see the most effective leaders function. They resist the idea of trying to change people or rushing out in front of the team with a flag yelling, 'Charge! We're going to change!' Instead, they create the conditions and an environment, as you say, for people to be great."

"That's an important distinction," Rachel replied. "When a culture has been established where a person's reputation has become more important than his or her character and values, you're going to have problems. It results in people not doing or saying the things that will expose them to the burden of blame for some potential error in judgment. The instant teammates choose not to be 'all in' by withholding information or effort, they marginalize their value to the organization. In that second, they forfeit their potential and what's possible because they've moved from wanting to do their best – to wanting to remain safe in the environment they're in."

"This means, of course, that it's not really about the team after all," I said. "It's about their personal safety. And when people act on their own self-interest, the organization underachieves. This is a common comment on our pre-session surveys."

Rachel shrugged her shoulders. "But you can't blame people. This is what I see many of my peers doing – bemoaning how no one is accountable, how no one is stepping up. And frankly, that's where I have a lot of work to do. I've got to partner with the other divisional heads so they realize that *they* need to step up as leaders and equip their team with the skill to be responsible. Complaining, pep talks, and rhetoric won't change how their team is behaving.

"An organization can't sustain a winning trend, can't expect people to be 'all in,' to give their best every day, only for a paycheck." Rachel sat back and laughed. "In so many cases, companies have trained people to pursue the carrot of a bigger paycheck or the corner office, which means the company then finds itself saddled with the burden of a huge payroll and thin margins. But they lack the one thing that will deliver exceptional, timely products to their customers: an *inspired* workforce, led by inspired people."

"Yes, and the transformation . . ." is all I could say before she cut me off.

"It's a fact: If you're going to win in the market today, you have to equip your team members with the tools and the mindset that allows them to live the values prized by them and the organization. Doing so provides them with the foundation to act now – rather than later. When you do that, watch out: You're going to see serious acceleration."

"Given how hard you've worked on this approach, what does that look like to you now, to 'allow them to live their values'?" I asked.

"Hey, people don't get out of bed each morning wanting to be irresponsible. Nobody wakes up and says, 'I can't wait to screw things up for everybody!'" Rachel said with a mock smile. "People don't want to go slow. These are good people we're talking about. Intellectually, everyone 'gets it.' But living and leading from your values is not an intellectual exercise. It's a function of your emotions and your company's culture. For example, most people have the desire to serve others. But if you don't put tools and a system in place for people to be emotionally intelligent *together*, the desire rarely transforms into action. This is when things begin to break down. And we all know how bad it can get."

I recalled the first discussion I'd had with Rachel. "I believe you told me once that you and the team 'delivered results despite yourselves.'"

Rachel nodded. "I remember that conversation," she said and then paused. "You know, I'm compelled to share some information with you now that I didn't tell you before. It will help put into greater context how much progress we've made."

I set my pen down and sat back.

"After I had been in this position for about a year," she continued, "there was a defining moment for this team. My boss was pushing us hard, and between you and me, placing unreasonable demands on us. I think there's a moment in every team's lifecycle when it's severely tested and the team has to decide: Are we going to do this thing? Are we going to be responsible and succeed? Because if we're not, it's going to be toilsome for all of us and probably end painfully.

"To make matters worse, my predecessor was like a terrorist – pardon the expression." Rachel shifted nervously in her chair. "I probably should find a better term to describe him. It's just that in his drive to succeed, because he was always focused on problems and talking consequences, he injected fear into the organization. People were running around here looking over their shoulders, avoiding the obvious, not saying what needed to be said nor doing what needed to be done.

"Don't get me wrong, though. People were working harder than they ever had, but our productivity wasn't improving. The issue wasn't a lack of effort – it was a breakdown in our 'values-to-action' capability." She paused and then added, "It was a breakdown in our responsibility to ourselves.

"And you know," Rachel said as she looked out her window, "I got sucked into it. For a while, I forfeited my values, set them aside. I became so driven by *what* had to be done that I valued the outcome more than the method by which we got there. I began to rationalize my poor behavior: 'If I'm going to be treated this way, then that's how I'm going to treat people.' It got so bad that when they told us about the drop in our employee engagement index, I coldly replied that those numbers would improve as soon as we returned to profitability." Rachel shook her head. "I felt justified for leading like a pain in the you know what."

I was deeply sympathetic. Her reaction to the intense pressures of the corporate world was normal. But she had survived and broken through to an improved approach. She could now speak clearly of the deep personal costs of winning in the short term by destroying that which is necessary for sustained growth: people . . . and the expression of greatness that resides in each of us.

"That's about the time I almost lost what I cherish the most." Rachel turned her gaze from the window and cleared her throat. "It was the middle of the week. I got home after my husband and the kids had finished dinner. I had the usual insane amount of communications to complete, and there was a report my boss needed that was giving me heartburn. I snapped at the kids, told them to clean up after themselves, and started for my computer. Things cascaded, one thing after another. My son said an awful thing about his sister and, of course, she had to respond with venom.

"So I yelled at them – really loud. And I was going to yell more when my husband spoke up and said, 'That's enough.'

"I thought he was talking to the kids. But when I looked at him, I knew in an instant it was me." Rachel looked at her hands. "And he was right. It was enough.

"That night my husband and I talked about what we'd been thinking – but not saying. The job, my work, was costing too much. The way we were living our lives was taking a toll that couldn't be paid. I was out of energy. And as I thought about my relationship with our kids . . ." Rachel shook her head. "How had I lost a proper perspective? When did I get so deep into this thing that it began consuming me?

"Our first solution was for me to quit my job. We dreamed a bit about what it might be like to simplify everything, but that was an empty fantasy. Something told us that quitting wasn't right. There were so many things about our life that we loved. We enjoyed the lifestyle, and – it was the first time I admitted this – I really *liked* the vision I had for my work. I told my husband there were aspects of leadership that were very fulfilling for me. I just didn't like how I was leading.

"I didn't sleep that night," she said. "In the morning, my husband looked at me over his coffee cup and suggested I call his uncle, Will. Perhaps he'd have some ideas." Rachel gestured toward me. "And you know the story from there, though I suspect you don't call him 'Uncle Will,' do you?"

I laughed. Will had been a client for years. As a CFO, he'd transformed two organizations with his innovative leadership style before retiring. "No, I don't call him 'Uncle Will,' but I am honored to consider him a friend," I said. "When I met with Will recently and told him I'd be seeing you again, he mentioned that he fondly recalled his conversation with you."

"It was the most important call I've ever made," Rachel said. "I described how tired I was, how miserable our family was, and how hard the team was working yet only accomplishing mediocre results. I shared my frustrations and how I just knew the team – especially I – was capable of doing so much more with our numbers.

"After listening, this man I didn't really know did something I didn't expect: He congratulated me. He said, 'You've reached the point everybody gets to. It's when you decide if you're going to change how you're creating change.'

"I guess my reaction was defensive," she said. "I shot back to clear the record of how there were others involved.

"'Yes,' he said. 'But will you be responsible *first*?' he asked. 'Or will you continue to be a victim of the illusion that you can change others without changing yourself and how you lead first?'

"Everything was quiet for a moment." Rachel smiled at me and said, "I have to tell you, initially I was put-off by his comment. He was telling me what I knew was true but didn't want to hear: I was responsible for the experience I was having – and the results I was delivering.

"Then he asked me, 'So, have you made a decision yet?'

"With that, we launched into a conversation I should have had a long time ago. And as we talked, he did something I'd never experienced before: He assisted me in answering the question of my own responsibility . . ." Rachel paused as she searched for the right words ". . . by pulling something from me that I vaguely recognized but had forgotten over the years."

"What was that?" I asked.

"It's the story about me that I stopped believing," she said. "As I spoke, I began to feel a confidence that I'd forgotten about."

I sat still for a moment, watching Rachel search for her words, and then asked, "Confidence to do what?"

"To start moving forward again. I began to remember that I am bigger than the circumstances in my life. I'm bigger than late reports. I'm bigger than production and quality issues. I'm bigger than kids fighting." She shrugged her shoulder. "I'm a bit embarrassed to say these things, because intellectually I *knew* all this. I just needed someone . . ." She chuckled. "I just needed someone to remind me, to ask me the right questions so I could return to the confidence necessary to do something about the circumstances in my life."

"You said he asked you questions. What type of questions?" I asked.

"A specific type of question that immediately guided my focus, generated momentum, and provided clarity on how to move forward," Rachel answered.

"At the end of that conversation, I asked Uncle Will, 'How did you learn to do this? How did you learn to lead like this?' And that's when he told me about the one thing – just one technique – that changes everything. That's when he told me about Degrees of Strength."

Will introduced Rachel and me – and we began immediately. I wasn't surprised to learn that Will was using Degrees of Strength to serve others in the transformation of their mindset and actions: He understood its principle that it is impossible for a person to have less than zero of any desired quality. And as you focus on the Degrees of Strength that are present in any given area – you accelerate the development of that quality.

Rachel's story also revealed that Will had used Degrees of Strength to form the questions he used to serve her. When people are asked such questions, they experience a realignment of their perspective – and a deeper connection to what's important. They are better able to regain their focus and take the steps necessary to move from clouds of chaotic confusion to deliver the excellence they long to realize. It's very exciting to be part of someone's life in this way. Like many, Rachel took to it with a ferocity that surprised family and colleagues.

"We haven't wasted any time since we first saw you," she said. "From the moment the team was introduced to this technique, we continue to advance our collective capability," Rachel said. She sat back, "I believe we've had our acceleration moment."

"That's a new way of saying it. Why do you use that?"

"It's the moment we became responsible. It's when we *really* started to get work done around here. It's when we decided to quit waiting for other people to change, or for the market or our resources to improve, or for our customers to quit being so fickle, before we acted. Basically, we stopped waiting for things to be different than they are in any given moment before doing what needed to be done."

She sat up, smiled slightly, and then said, "Personally, the acceleration moment is when I became responsible for the experience I was having. I took charge of my reactions to everything that was happening around me. That's when I began to enjoy my job again. I got back to that mindset where work wasn't work. And when this happened . . ." Rachel's voice fell off.

"You started getting better results?" I asked.

"Of course," she said with a slow nod. "But more importantly, I got my family back."

CHAPTER TWO

Case Study: Changing the Approach to Change

Rachel had quickly grasped the role of an Accelerator.

What's more, if her team can coordinate and align, they have the potential to be another "worst to first" case study: taking their organization from muddling in the "nowhere lane" to setting the standard for their company or industry.

Accelerators earn this name because they're about speed with connotations of efficiency, brevity, focus, and the ability to deliver something sooner than otherwise possible. In short, Accelerators get those around them to the point of realized potential *quicker*. As in the chemistry of mixing adhesive, an accelerator is often added to quicken the dry time; therefore, it's a catalyst for producing a finished product in a faster time. This enhances stability. Additionally, an accelerator inhibits other elements from interfering. This stability yields profits and is the backbone of the change effort.

Leaders who are Accelerators transform what people can do. They do this everywhere they go, in every interaction: emphasize the *most* effective method of improving performance – immediately and long term. And the most effective technique is to leverage the Degrees of Strength that are present in every person and situation.

Accelerators can be found at every level within your organization, influencing others vertically and horizontally. Furthermore, not all those in leadership positions are Accelerators. But, they can learn to become one.

What does it look like when leaders and their teams use Degrees of Strength to transform performance? Because Accelerators don't boast, we'll brag for them: Meet Rich, a senior-level leader of a multinational corporation. Rich found himself in Geneva, Switzerland, after his company purchased its largest European competitor.

"The line of sight to success was clear to me," he said. "But so what if the project leader can see what needs to be done? Nothing significant is going to happen until everyone is tightly aligned on the same vision, has the foundation of trust, and is communicating well. So creating the right environment for change became the immediate priority."

Rich has long understood the power of an inspired workforce. He and I have talked about how its magic is far removed from direct orders and monetary baiting. His new leadership situation was about integration and developing an "ownership mindset" – qualities beyond the limits of old-school, top-down leadership methods.

"To be honest, this was a stretch assignment for me. We had an organization where leaders were coming from seven different countries. Forget about the personality differences – we all saw our world differently! Immediately, we focused on leveraging our collective know-how so we could create a new culture.

"Our mission was to align our two companies so we could optimize operations and capture the synergies we had committed to the corporation. This meant merging twenty of our current manufacturing plants with the nineteen acquired plants, along with all the support functions. And, of course, during this entire time we had to service and satisfy our customers.

"We had committed to three-year targets to complete many of these programs. The pressure to perform was unlike anything I had experienced before in my career. My first impulse was to move *too* fast and use the outdated default approach by telling the team:

- 'Here's the vision.' (Translation to team: I don't care what you see.)
- 'I have the solutions.' (You don't.)
- 'Here's what you have to do.' (What you're doing isn't working.)
- 'And here's why we have to get it done.' (Your priorities are less important.)"

While often a natural impulse, the liabilities of this old leadership style are well documented. Rich and other Accelerators call it the degrees of weakness approach because it tells the team "You're not capable. You don't possess the strength necessary to succeed." High-performance leaders know this is the polar opposite mindset with which they want their teams approaching their job. ("You're not capable . . . now go forth and be responsible.")

"How do you change people's thinking – their mindset? You tell them what to think and do, right?" he said. "Because this approach is so common, it's tempting to fall prey to using it. I still slip occasionally and try to persuade others with my righteous and rational thinking," Rich laughed. "But my wife will tell you that my success rate with that method is zero."

Instead of blasting them with the "we bought you" mentality, Rich deliberately practiced restraint. "I knew if we were going to ask these leaders to respond to a changing business model, then we'd first have to be clear on expectations, include them in the process, and make them part of building the future. Also, if we were going to drive this extraordinary change, we'd have to change how we were all showing up for work. And if you're going to change behaviors, you have to affect the mindset."

At that point, Rich was in the leadership moment when a person can change the trajectory of an entire organization. "We had to change how we approach change. Equipping the leadership team with the skill to be able to do this made the difference. Immediately – and together – we moved to:

- 'Here's the vision . . . What do we – together – see and believe is possible?'
- 'Here's what we have to accomplish . . . What are we collectively doing that's already working, and what efforts created that?'
- 'These are the solutions we see from our perspective . . . What experience, wisdom and ideas within the region can we better leverage?'
- 'And here's why we have to get it done . . . Why, at a local level, do you want to see this plan succeed?'"

The contrast between these two approaches hardly requires explanation. The first approach is like an impersonal recorded voice through a bullhorn. The second approach is where Rich uses the Degrees of Strength technique. This allows the employees to leverage their successes and use their hard-earned experience in developing the vision and action to move forward, accelerating from "you vs. me" – to "us" and "team."

"I've always believed that the best leadership is selfless. To get the results the company wants, the focus must be on the people performing the work," said Rich. "When you facilitate their greatness, you bring the best people have to offer into their everyday actions. And when this happens you not only get up the mountain, you can move the mountain."

This is what Rich's team did. They succeeded by delivering before the time targeted, and the rewards came in more ways than just positive numbers. "Around the holidays, we went to tour a plant," Rich recalled. "There in the entryway was a flag with our company logo flying next to their country flag. The entire team was there and greeted us with smiles and handshakes. I knew then: We were making a difference. The company culture was evolving."

As this book was being written, a call came from a client who is a VP for a large food and beverage company. Her words reveal even more clearly why Accelerators are able to transform what people can do by using Degrees of Strength: "Greatness – the ability to think and do extraordinary things – resides in each of us. We know that about *ourselves*. But what remains necessary for organizations to perform significantly better is for more people to know that this fact is also true about the people *around us*. There's incredible potential within everyone. Therefore, what's needed is a construct, a way of seeing and being in everyday interactions that allows us to live and lead with that greatness more consistently. That tool is Degrees of Strength."

Imagine a day when more leaders have the skill to lead their teams to greater results in a way that enriches the lives of every team member. This is the promise of Degrees of Strength: It develops capabilities and performance faster than anything else because it's a mechanism to call the potential that so many mistakenly think resides outside of people or in the future . . . into now, into reality.

(Why wait to be great when we can be great now?)

CHAPTER THREE

Roberto: The Degrees of Strength Move from Red to Green

Rachel is genuine. When you speak with her, you feel as though you are her top priority. Our conversation provided an insight into the transformation she was making – yet the real test remained.

"In what ways do you see the team successfully integrating this new approach in its daily work?" I asked.

Rachel grinned and said, "Rather than tell you, I'd like you to experience it." Her smile grew bigger. "You remember Roberto from our session? Go and talk with him. He played a critical role in our acceleration moment. If he hadn't started using Degrees of Strength, we wouldn't be having this conversation right now." She turned to her computer screen, and then with a playful shake of her finger and cheerful admonishment said, "But whatever you do, don't tell him he's being positive."

Roberto is tall and, with his hand thrust toward me from the other side of his desk, he's imposing. It's also easy to understand why he's in charge of operations: After shaking hands, he sat down and got to the point quickly. "Rachel probably sent you to my office because it took me so long to understand what you were all talking about," Roberto said. "Let's face it, the Degrees of Strength approach isn't the normal way of doing things." His expression was grim after saying this . . . and then a gentle smile crossed his face.

"I've been through every corporate training on the planet, and they always come down to attitude – just be *positive!*" Roberto said with hands held up in feigned delight. "Initially, after we went through your session, I saw Degrees of Strength like that. But I noticed that most everyone else was moving things forward faster and I was still stuck in mounting frustrations."

"Then why is it Rachel told me you were the most important person to influence the team's acceleration?" I asked.

"She said that?" He puffed his chest slightly, holding the compliment for a moment to enjoy it.

"Yes," I said. "Each team seems to have a pivotal person who significantly subtracts or adds to the momentum. And it sounds like you are the one."

"Whatever," Roberto said, still holding a slight grin. "I can tell you the precise moment when I finally grasped this Degrees of Strength paradigm. It was on our family trip to . . . what are they called? The Black Hills?" He turned and picked up a framed photo of his family standing in front of a large cave. "Yes, it's in South Dakota, the Wind Cave they call it. One of the longest caves in the world. Our tour guide led us down hundreds of feet into the earth. The maze of tunnels was crazy with tight spots and water dripping everywhere. It's really dark down there and you wear huge headlamps to see. But it was still difficult because shadows were dancing everywhere. It really spooked my kids. As if that weren't disorienting enough, after we'd walked an hour – I tell you, I felt as if we were in the belly of the earth – the guide turned and asked, 'Are you ready?'

"We all stopped and wondered, 'Ready for what?'"

"'Okay, turn off your lights,' the guide said.

"Instantly everything went black. *Real* black. *Todo negro*. I rubbed my eyes and strained, searching for something to see. I put my hand directly in front of my face, but there was nothing.

"What the guide said next helped me understand how you talk about Degrees of Strength. 'If you're waiting for your eyes to adapt,' said the guide, 'you'll have to wait a long time because there's no light for your eyes to adjust to. There is zero light here. It can't get any darker than this.'

"It was almost suffocating standing in that blackness. Then, one of my children clicked on their lamp. And then on came another, and slowly, that dark cavern began to fill with light." The large man sat back and put his hands behind his head and smiled. "That's when I understood the power of this tool."

"Understood what, exactly?" I asked, wanting him to make the connection clear.

Roberto shot forward, planting his large hands on his desk. "Just as you said: You can't have less than zero of any quality! There's either complete darkness – or there are degrees of light. And with every incremental increase of light, your eyes adjust and you can see more."

I didn't want to insult Roberto but couldn't help asking, "How's that different from what you were doing before?"

He slowly rubbed his fingers across the surface of the desk. "As you informed us, my friend, Degrees of Strength show up in everything. After hearing that there's nothing less than complete darkness, I could see your point applied to other areas. For example, how do you measure how cold something is? By degrees of heat, of course. I looked it up on Wikipedia and found that everything is measured from an absolute zero, that's called Kelvin, which is something like -273 degrees Celsius. It's impossible to go below zero degrees kelvin. You can't have less than no heat. Just like we couldn't have less than no light in that cave, the same goes for heat. There is either no heat or increasing degrees of heat.

"You've taken this in a nice direction," I said.

"Ah, but here's the big rub, mi amigo," Roberto said as he gently raised his hand. "It was only after I saw how we use this principle in the measuring of light or temperature that I realized how it applies as we interact with other people. As likely as not, we measure others by the *illusion* of degrees of weakness." He leaned forward. "We pretend someone has less than zero of what is needed to move forward."

Roberto stood up. "Have you ever heard people say something like, 'Nobody is accountable around here' or 'We can never seem to deliver on time' or –" he stopped and started laughing.

"Why is that so funny?" I asked, trying to keep up with him.

"No, no, it's my wife," Roberto answered. "She's taking voice lessons, and I hear her say, 'My singing is so bad!' And I remind her, 'Mi amor! I hear nothing but beauty in your songs!' And it's true, because I see the strengths in what she is singing to the world." He leaned closer to me. "Can you imagine what will happen to her experience – her *voice* – when she sees her own singing in Degrees of Strength like I do?"

"So, just by being positive you –"

"Don't give me that!" Roberto interrupted, his voice booming. He dropped into his chair and put his fist on the desk. "If I tell my team 'just be positive,' it might brighten their day, but it doesn't move us forward."

I sat back and gave him room. I love where and how far people take these ideas.

He pointed out his window. "Do you know how many people out there are trying to be positive – but they don't get a darn thing done all day? Too many. And on top of that –" He interrupted himself by pushing a button on his phone. It beeped and he half-yelled into the phone, "Bernie, bring the production numbers from last month in here." He let go of the button, looked at me, and then pressed the button again. "Please." Roberto crossed his arms and said, "I'm going to show you what this looks like in action."

Almost instantly, a middle-aged, blonde, and stoic-looking man entered the office. "Hello, Bernie. Good to see you again," I said.

"You, too," Bernie nodded. He had multiple charts flapping in his hand.

"On the table, Bernie," Roberto said as he walked toward the corner of the room. Together they unfolded the charts, full of bar graphs colored in red, yellow, and green. Roberto pointed at them and asked, "What do you see?"

A bit uncertain as to what angle he was driving at, I said, "Um, your production scores?"

"Si! They are our scores. And what color do you notice first?"

I looked at the charts and it jumped out at me. "Red."

"Red! Red! Red – it represents the places we are not performing on target. It's a bright reminder of all the places we fall short in our systems. And there's too much red! That's my point, you see?"

I stared blankly at him.

"Red is not *positive*," Roberto said. "There's nothing about red that makes me feel good. There's nothing about red that makes me want to say, 'Oh, it's going to be all right.' If I walk out of this office whistling a tune and tell the team 'just be positive,' they'll laugh me out of the meeting – and the board of execs will have my head on a platter.

"But!" Roberto held his finger high. "When I use Degrees of Strength, then I have my . . . my . . ." He put his finger down and turned to Bernie. "What does Rachel call it? The moment?"

"Then we have our *acceleration moment*," Bernie answered.

"She told me about this," I told them. "And I have to say I like it. We've heard different names for it."

Bernie looked at Roberto, as if to ask, "May I?"

Roberto nodded and we all sat next to the colored charts. Bernie, sitting straight, continued. "What is working for Roberto with this method of analysis is that it isn't about focusing on the positive. Instead, we focus on the strengths that *do* exist – even in the red areas."

"Yeah, you don't have to ignore the reality of the situation – like cheerleaders of the losing team in the last minutes of the game," said Roberto. "Red is red, and we better understand quickly why it is red."

"What you have shown us, or the part that works especially well for us, is now we transition rather quickly into a problem-solving mindset that generates momentum," said Bernie, tapping the charts. "And sometimes it seems these charts turn red overnight. For us, the speed is essential."

"We now know this means the speed with which we can create the *conditions* that generate greater profits," Roberto added. "That mindset is completely different than what I was thinking earlier in my career."

I leaned forward and said, "Assist me in understanding specifically how this is making a difference for you."

Without warning, something buzzed in Roberto's coat pocket. He pulled out his phone and with rapt attention began texting. Bernie looked at his boss and then pulled one of the charts closer. "What made sense to me is when you talked about how our brain manages to process thoughts in any given moment."

"How your mind is working *all the time*," Roberto injected, without looking up from his phone.

Bernie nodded and said, "The tool, '3 Mind Factors,' that you gave us gradually made more sense." He pulled a card out of his pocket and held it like a badge in front of me:

3 Mind Factors

1) You can only focus on one thought at a time.
2) You can't avoid a "don't."
3) You go in the direction of your focus.

"We leverage these as often as we can," Bernie continued. "Here's a perfect example of the first one: Your mind can only focus on one thought at a time." Bernie looked nervously at Roberto. "Roberto is either listening to comprehend what we're discussing or he's reading to understand his texts. He may be able to go back and forth between the two thoughts extremely fast, but he can't focus on both at the same time."

Bernie stopped and waited for Roberto's response, but his eyes remained glued on his phone. Bernie looked at me with raised eyebrows, as if to say, "See?"

I smiled and then asked him, "How about the second Mind Factor: You can't avoid a 'don't' message or focus. How have you incorporated that?"

Bernie almost seemed to laugh. "It's easy to understand that you can't avoid a message built on 'don't' statements, but I have to tell you, this old habit is deeply engrained. Just the other day I finished a meeting and told the crew, 'Don't blow your production numbers this month.' And as soon as I said it, I knew I blew it. Guess what they walked out of the room focused on?"

"Blowing their production numbers this month," I answered.

"Exactly!" Roberto said, as he seemed to suddenly wake up. "But it took some time to understand how deep that approach runs in me. I used to constantly tell people what I didn't want them to do. I specifically focused their attention on what I didn't want to see happen, leaving them stranded there." He shook his head. "People weren't irresponsible because they wanted to be. They seemed irresponsible, sure enough, but often because I led them to a counterproductive focus and marooned them there." He returned his phone to the holster on his belt and said, "No wonder Rachel wanted to get rid of me."

I looked back at Bernie. He broke into a slight grin and then said, "After accepting the first two Mind Factors, the third Mind Factor – you go in the direction of your focus – cinches the deal. Instead of pummeling the team with 'don't do this' and 'don't blow that,' we work harder at providing the path in which we want to go. This becomes extremely important when you add it to the first Mind Factor – whatever thought my focus is on, that's the direction I'm going."

Roberto interrupted. "Correction. That's the direction your entire team is going." He shook his head and then looked up at me. "Only after I got these 3 Mind Factors right did I get Degrees of Strength right."

I sat still for a moment, very interested in how yet another team showed me new insights into this fundamental understanding. I pointed to one of the red bars. "Tell me how you are applying the Degrees of Strength technique here."

"When we break things down with the 3 Mind Factors, it becomes very clear," Bernie answered. "It's so automatic, like a reflex, to assess our abilities or progress in terms of how poorly we are performing. And if that's my focus, and because I go in the direction of my focus, guess where we spend our energy?" Bernie looked over at Roberto and added, "Which direction do I take my team?"

"Absolutely right," Roberto said. He looked up. "The way I used to message to my team – I was loco. I would say, 'We're not making any progress' and 'We've got to stop screwing up!' and 'We never listen to our customers.' Those were like maxims for me." He leaped out of his chair and began to pace. "And then I'd double down on the team. I'd ask legendary questions based on degrees of weakness, just to ensure I slowed my team down even more. 'Who's making these mistakes?' 'Why are these problems still problems?' 'Why can't we move this forward?'"

Roberto laughed so loud that Bernie and I looked at each other. Then he added, "What I didn't know really hurt me. Hurt *us*. They couldn't move things forward because of my focus, which I had given to them. As I was glued on the degrees of where we were weak, I was expanding those weaknesses. I was leading them backward. They followed my orders and I blamed them for it."

Roberto suddenly stopped, stared at us with big eyes, and said, "I have to tell you, mis amigos, it was a significant blow to my ego when I realized my leadership was actually backfiring. Rachel talks about leading so we discover the greatness within people, so we can release the potential they have." He shook his head. "I was so worried about my greatness that I hadn't even considered theirs."

"It makes you wonder how you made it this far, doesn't it?" I said.

Roberto scowled at me, and Bernie put his head down. A momentary silence filled the room – long enough for me to second-guess why I had attempted the joke.

"I was managing the best way I knew how. It's the way I learned how to do it. Never in a million years would I have thought my leadership was hurting people and performance," Roberto said as his scowl faded and he returned to his seat. "Rachel was always insisting that we speak up and take greater responsibility. And I was! But every time I spoke up, her hair seemed to stand on end. You could see she was frustrated with me."

"I don't understand how you could affect her like that," I said. "What were you saying – and what did you learn from that?"

"She said she needed the facts. And that's what I gave her," Roberto answered. "It took me a while to learn that yes, she wanted the facts – but *how* those facts were interpreted and used was the leadership difference she was looking for."

"Tell me more," I said.

"Because all the information I was sharing was built to place blame or skirt responsibility with excuses. I used to share facts from a degrees of weakness perspective, so everything was interpreted or understood with a destructive or limiting energy: 'Here's where we're in trouble.' 'These are all the problems we have.' 'We'll never have enough resources.' I was Mr. Doom and Gloom," Roberto said.

"Your analysis of the data was right on the mark – you just had your aim skewed," I said.

"When I discovered that you can take the same numbers, the same facts, and see and use them differently – well, it changed everything. After coming back from that dark cave we visited on our vacation, I began speaking up with, 'Here's why we can close that gap.' 'These are the conditions we must create to generate solutions.' 'Here are the options our resources currently provide us.'"

"Rachel's interpretation of responsibility," Bernie spoke up, "isn't asking us to fall on the sword or point out who's to blame. This paradigm of Degrees of Strength has fueled an acceptance of responsibility, because now there's always something we can stand on to gain traction forward. There's always a strength to build on. And it's taking us beyond simply being engaged as employees. Now, it's about ownership – owning where we are and owning the path forward in a way that builds people, partnerships, and performance."

Looking directly at Roberto, I said, "I appreciate your candidness. It sounds as though your language changed."

"Not just mine," said Roberto. "Our organizational language is changing. And this means we can move faster together."

Bernie cleared his throat and said, "By the way, I wouldn't say Rachel's hair stands on end anymore. Since our acceleration moment, how she leads us has changed, too."

"Yes. You're right," Roberto said with a slight nod to Bernie. "It's interesting. Until you said that, I would have never realized how much Rachel has shifted to seeing me in Degrees of Strength. When she first got here, I could tell she was trying to fix me, as if I were broken. Every time we talked, it was a constant barrage of 'here's-what-you're-doing-wrong' messages.

"Honestly, it was getting to the point where I was almost hoping she'd fail." He stopped, then looked directly at me and added, "I said *almost*."

It was quiet for a moment. Then Roberto grunted and said, "You know, I hadn't thought about that until now. A lot of times people think they have a personnel issue, when in reality they have a leadership issue."

"It's a critical difference," I said. "One more of us should consider."

"About the time we started learning the Degrees of Strength approach is the same time Rachel changed from trying to change me – to changing how she communicated with me. Rather than telling me what to do, she . . ." he paused. "She began to shift my mindset, how I was *seeing* things – knowing that if my focus changed, my thoughts and actions would change."

"So how did this shift in thinking change how you see the charts?" I asked.

Bernie picked up his pen and drew a familiar line on the paper and then marked it with numbers.

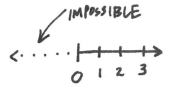

"How we use the 3 Mind Factors to assess information is when we determine which direction we're going – and the types of results we'll accelerate," Bernie said, sounding like a professor. "The truth is, it's impossible to have less than zero of what we need to succeed. So, in these red areas here," he pointed at the chart, "once you understand the data, you can then understand what has to happen to succeed. But rather than working backward from your objective, with Degrees of Strength, you determine what you need to do more of, in addition to, or better to achieve your objective. If you lose your focus on these areas of strength, you do so at your team's peril," Bernie said with another look toward Roberto.

Roberto glanced at his numbers guy with a blank expression and then turned to me and said, "I don't blame him. Because all I used in the past was a degrees of weakness approach, I was constantly focused on what wasn't happening. This meant every change required extraordinary effort. Every day was a grind because the only momentum we had was backward. And because that approach automatically lowered performance, I then defaulted into thinking I had to become tougher. I had to become more demanding. I had to make sure they knew how badly they were performing."

He shrugged his shoulders and continued. "My intentions were good. But I'd become so controlling, I think team members were beginning to interpret my actions as if I didn't care about them. This frustration – mine and theirs – generated indifference within the team, and ultimately, it created the opposite of what we were trying to build: a workforce willing to go beyond engagement."

"Most of us depend on our well-honed problem-solving skills to successfully negotiate our daily work," Bernie said as if to throw his boss a lifeline. "It's about root-cause analysis and everything else we learned in school, right? Our professions stand on it. Yet, we have to use these skills judiciously. If we study our challenges and issues in a way that tears people down and corrodes partnership, you can predict that poor performance will follow. Sometimes you don't have to say a word and people can sense it. Even the most sincere desires to help people move things forward can inadvertently cause harm.

"This is when leaders fear losing control, like Rachel's predecessor," Bernie continued. "After dismantling our innate desire to do great work, he'd then go through Olympian-like efforts to motivate us to better performance. He'd send out positive emails and have HR plaster the walls with inspirational posters. But while the hallways were filled with greetings and nervous smiles, behind closed doors, people were talking about finding a better job. If people use only positive pleasantries and platitudes, the depth of their actions – or lack thereof – will always out them. You can smile, but if you're using degrees of weakness, few will follow."

"I've got to tell you," Roberto said as he looked back at the graph. "As I grasp this Degrees of Strength technique, I feel invigorated as a leader unlike anything I've known before. I never realized how the daily study of how terrible we were as a team was hardening me. The callousness in my approach was pickling how I saw everything. In contrast, this study of excellence – our own excellence – revives me. It makes me feel like I did when I was younger, as though there are only possibilities ahead."

The thoughtful man in front of me had a momentary expression on his face that seemed to melt barriers. He pulled off his glasses, put one of the stems gently in his mouth, and said, "I still don't truly understand why we're successful in many of these green areas on the chart." He looked at Bernie. "If I do a better job of helping our team understand what's working well in our areas of green results, then we can replicate those practices in the areas of red. Perhaps that can assist us in being more responsible in the areas we need it most."

Roberto stopped while Bernie wrote some notes. Then he continued, "But, like I said, it takes time to develop new habits. I'm still drawn to the urgency of these red scores. At least by using Degrees of Strength I'm accelerating those from red to yellow and –" He stopped again and pointed at a green line. "Just one month ago this score was red, and Bernie, what were those five questions we used to create a new focus and follow-up plan?"

Bernie pulled another card out of his pocket. "It's the 'Recipe for Partnership.'"

Recipe for Partnership

1) What's working well in this area right now?
2) What created those successes?
3) What are our objectives?
4) Why are accomplishing those objectives important?
5) What can we do more of, in addition to, or better to achieve our objectives?"

"A year ago, I could have never accelerated that red to green so fast," Roberto said. "It kills me knowing that in every tough issue I've faced in my life, every red score I've ever seen, there were strengths just lying there dormant, waiting for me to focus on them, be responsible, and activate a forward momentum."

"Yes, and don't forget to celebrate yourself," I said. "Remember, you are the one who created it."

"Perhaps I should lighten up a bit," he said. "Make no mistake: We're all after positive outcomes. You can hardly argue with the benefits of 'being a positive person,' but as a leadership strategy, that approach leans dangerously close to employing wishful thinking as a means to improving performance. Degrees of Strength gives us a method to address the issues, even the nasty, ugly ones, by developing our capability to be more responsible."

CHAPTER FOUR

Case Study: Execution and Excellence – Even in Tough Situations

Accelerators aren't necessarily optimists; they might call themselves realists. (Roberto wouldn't consider himself a saint.) But because Accelerators focus on the Degrees of Strength in every person and situation, they quickly become optimistic.

There's a subtle difference there – and Accelerators ensure their team members see it: Those who lead from degrees of weakness wait for success to materialize before becoming optimistic. Accelerators *create* momentum toward the next success by focusing on where strengths and success already exist. Accelerators see the red smeared all over the chart and interpret it as opportunities. (To be sure, they don't dance around the office yelling, "Yippee! Everything is great!" Instead, it shows up with a determined "We can do this" message to the team.) With this outlook, Accelerators gain a reputation for accountability. They can be found in the toughest situations working with passion and the ability to execute toward resolution.

Roberto, then, increasingly models the Degrees of Strength technique:

1. Operating from the paradigm and wisdom that it's impossible to have less than zero of any desired quality or characteristic.
2. Being disciplined in the focus on the strengths that exist in every person and situation.
3. Leveraging and acting upon those strengths to accelerate forward.

A client of ours, John, is a manager within a Fortune Global 50 company. He provides an example of what this technique looks like in action. In the case study that follows, to accomplish the third step in the Degrees of Strength technique, he uses another tool that, just as with the 3 Mind Factors, has the ability to transform outcomes.

To position and understand the power of this next tool, try this: Stop reading for a moment and ask someone near you, "What time is it?" Then, observe what happens to his or her focus. Undoubtedly, almost instinctively, the focus shifts to determining what time it is.

The human mind can rarely resist a well-timed, well-phrased question. In other words, as soon as someone is asked a question, the mind becomes pointed in the direction of the focus presented. Therefore, questions become a trigger for reinforcing or establishing a new focus.

It even works when you use it on yourself. Choose a question – What do I want to eat for dinner? What do I want to accomplish as a leader? – and watch what happens to your focus.

Accelerators like John, below, understand the power of this tool, so they have a heightened awareness about what type of questions they're asking:

Backward focus questions create and reinforce a degrees of weakness paradigm. Used consistently, they weaken a person's or team's ability to move forward. Here are some examples:
- Why do we keep making these mistakes?
- What am I doing wrong?
- How did we fail to deliver quality?

Forward Focus Questions reinforce that there are Degrees of Strength present, trigger focus forward, and assist people in accelerating. Examples include:

- What do we need to do to improve?
- What can I do better?
- How can we ensure greater quality?

Forward Focus Questions, based on the fundamental understanding that Questions Trigger the Mind, are the most powerful tools there are to shift focus forward – and expand the Degrees of Strength inherent in any situation.

Accelerators don't stop there: Forward Focus Questions by themselves are effective at accelerating performance; when multiple Forward Focus Questions are placed in a certain order, the effect is exponential. This is accomplished by the Recipe for Partnership, which Bernie read from a card in Chapter Three. John shows how he strategically used this tool to save an account – and build the bottom line.

"We were pioneering an endeavor involving highly regarded community-based pharmacies, grocery chains, and community-based cancer centers. If successful, the potential was significant and would generate north of $800,000 annually in new business. The future success of this endeavor hinged upon the success of the pilot program.

"The pilot didn't go as planned. By all measures, the follow-up meeting with the stakeholders was poised for an unfavorable outcome. We were at risk of the customer disengaging and abandoning our pilot initiative based upon the dismal start. The temptation to lose our optimism was strong."

This is what is often missed in the description of an achiever's mindset. It is not unlike the mental training a top-ranking athlete or musician must have. Regardless of the skill, be it playing football or the violin, the Accelerator seeks to magnify the advantages and shore up the liabilities. You can't have it all, but a winning attitude requires honesty in assessing the reality and then moving forward with a competitive mindset of excellence. John's able to do this.

"Recognizing the gravity of the situation, I needed to do more than just show up on time for this pivotal meeting," said John. "I determined to keep the agenda for this pilot review grounded in Degrees of Strength. I would accomplish that by using a version of the Recipe for Partnership. Here's the agenda we used:

Agenda for Pilot Follow-Up Discussion Questions:

1. What is our progress to date?
2. What factors are contributing to existing successes?
3. What do we need to accomplish now?
4. What's the value of that to the program?
5. What are our next steps?"

John used the Recipe for Partnership as a template to ensure each question in the agenda built upon the momentum established by the previous focus:

- The first question establishes the existing progress (providing traction for forward progress).
- The second question identifies the processes that are functioning in their favor (so they're studying their own excellence instead of failure).
- The third step aligns commonly held objectives (shifting the mindset

focus of problems and what's not working to instead, where they need to go).

- The fourth question establishes a connection to purpose (thereby tapping into motivations – a key in any change effort).
- The fifth step ensures they move step-by-step toward those goals in a pragmatic manner.

Nothing complicated about it. Yet the Recipe for Partnership effectively brought John and the team success.

"Notwithstanding the gravity of the situation, the Degrees of Strength approach engaged the customer on a higher level – and we created a partnership. This retained the customer's commitment, underscored our collective vision, and maintained the customer's continued support of the pilot, which may have otherwise come to a complete and tragic end," he said.

"It's hard to imagine what might have been lost if I had used degrees of weakness by focusing first upon all that was wrong, thus overshadowing all that was going well. We've now strategically orchestrated a foundation that suggests success is more likely than failure. Not only is the pilot worthy of our continued efforts, the initiative may take on a whole new dimension, becoming self-sustaining and making a profound difference for cancer patients within the community. That's our evolving plan."

There is nothing like the wellspring of optimism – for any leader, and more importantly, for those you are influencing. And, as John reminds us, it's not necessary for things to be going *our* way in order to be optimistic. Optimism is a function of our ability to see what seems to be in the way – and using Degrees of Strength to transform the obstacle into a lever.

CHAPTER FIVE

Andrea: A Leader Gets Over Herself

Bernie walked out of Roberto's office with the charts under his arm. Roberto closed the door and said, "So . . . who else are you going to speak with on your visit? What skeletons are you looking for today?"

"Well, I'm certainly not searching for skeletons, and I'm not sure who I'll have an opportunity to speak with," I answered.

"Well, it's just that . . ." Roberto said and paused. "I'm not the most popular person here. If you talk to others, you're going to hear some crazy things."

"Is what they say true?" I asked.

Roberto chuckled as if he were reminding himself of something, put his hand on the doorknob, and said, "I suppose, yes. But the truth in degrees of weakness – and the truth in Degrees of Strength – has two different effects." He pulled the door open. "Let's just say I used to think that becoming a team player was a matter of commitment. Now, I've learned that it is also a skill. And I'm still a student."

We shared a laugh. I shook his hand and then made my way out to the hall. The day was still young, so I turned toward Rachel's office. Little did I know, Rachel could read minds: We nearly collided.

"Hello!" she said with a smile. "I was hoping to find you. How was your experience with Roberto?"

Surprised, I said, "Rachel – hi – yes. Roberto's working hard. You can tell he's making progress in moving what he has in his head into his actions. With continued discipline, he's got an opportunity to transform his leadership – and his results."

"Good. That sounds about right," Rachel said, putting her arm out and behind me to gently shepherd me the opposite direction. "I've just cancelled my ten o'clock meeting so I can introduce you to Andrea, our technology lead." We made our way onto an elevator and Rachel added, "You're going to love her – she's a pistol."

I was looking forward to this meeting, as I had not met Andrea in our original session.

Soon we were at the door, and after a light rap, Rachel pushed forward. The office was decadent – and behind the desk stood a short woman speaking curtly into her cell phone.

Andrea looked at us, silently pointed at her phone, rolled her eyes, and then turned away. Respecting her need for privacy, we stayed near the door. Rachel leaned her head toward me and whispered, "Andrea's the smartest person on the team. In fact, I don't know if I've ever worked with someone who has such a high IQ."

"That's great," I whispered back.

"Well, yes – and no. Intelligence is only part of the equation. It wasn't until she *applied* her intelligence that we started coming together and getting things done," Rachel said.

I looked at Andrea, who was talking sternly into the phone. There was no denying it: She had an intimidating energy. "What is the most important value she brings to the organization?" I asked in a low voice.

"You mean besides her intelligence?" Rachel asked. "Then it would have to be her high expectations for how we perform. She's relentless."

"That's a terrific quality," I said.

"Well, yes – and no," Rachel said again. "Andrea's still learning that having high expectations doesn't do anything for us if she's not helping us *realize* those expectations. Just because you've 'got it' doesn't make you valuable to our organization until you lead in a way where others 'get it.' And, truly, she's made great progress with that."

"How so?" I asked.

"Primarily in how she communicates with others. Our old degrees of weakness approach meant that her communications were intended for two purposes: search and destroy. In other words, all you got from Andrea was clarity around where you were underperforming and all the ways you weren't adding value." Rachel shook her head slightly. "Most people would rather have a root canal at the dentist than a meeting with Andrea, which meant it took forever to get any work done. But now we're seeing a lot more –" Rachel cut off her words as Andrea tossed her cell phone onto the desk.

"Hello, sorry about that. I'm Andrea," she said, motioning us forward to the front of her desk. "Please, have a seat. It's a pleasure to meet you at last."

Andrea had participated in a subsequent session, after the initial program I had facilitated. "The pleasure is mine," I said. "Thanks for allowing us some time. This follow-up work is essential."

After introductions, Rachel said, "I can only stay for a bit, but wanted to jump-start the conversation before leaving."

"Fine," Andrea said with a half smile. She took a quick glance at her watch and asked, "What have you already learned about our progress?"

After making myself comfortable in the seat, I answered, "I just had a wonderful conversation with Roberto, and it appears the team is developing an important collective awareness."

"Awareness!" she said with an exaggerated laugh. "I'm sure Roberto had some real productive things to say about me."

I wasn't sure if this was a question or a statement and looked at Rachel for guidance. When no assistance was offered, I turned back and said, "Well, actually, he didn't mention your name. We just talked about the progress he's making in his leadership by using the Degrees of Strength technique."

"Progress? Mr. 'Red-You're-Dead' thinks he's making progress?" Andrea said, raising her arms in mock surprise. Then her eyes moved to Rachel, who made an obvious display of moving forward in her chair.

"I missed the conversation, but I'm sure it was a good one," Rachel said. "What sort of progress do you see Roberto making that's important to you, Andrea?"

Andrea sat still for a moment and then took a breath. Pointing at her supervisor, she looked at me and said, "She's good, isn't she?" She grinned at Rachel. "You're right. You're right. I slipped." Then she turned to me and said, "Your time with me will probably provide you with a model of what *not* to do in leadership."

"That's okay, as long as we see it contrasted with what *to* do," Rachel said.

Andrea stared blankly at her boss for a moment and then said, "That's fair." She paused. "Roberto has begun to include me on more communications – particularly around organizational strategy – much sooner. This is helping my team do its job faster."

Rachel, her face serious, sat back and said, "That's Degrees of Strength in action."

"Sure," Andrea answered. "And what I still struggle with is he could – he should – be doing so much more."

"And how does that 'struggle' affect your work, your leadership?" Rachel asked.

Andrea contemplated this a moment, looked at me, stood up, and moved over to her window. "I know you're here to follow up on what we are doing, but I want to change this conversation before we go somewhere we shouldn't."

"What's important for you to say?" I asked.

"This whole Degrees of Strength technique is partly inspiring me – and partly driving me crazy," she said as she crossed her arms. "It's inspiring because I've never found such a powerful approach to getting to where I want to go as a leader, to being the type of leader I've always wanted to be."

"And it's driving you crazy?" Rachel asked with an understanding tone.

"Because . . ." her voice slowed as she formulated her thoughts. "Because I don't feel like I'm making progress.

"So, if you don't mind, I'd just like to tell you what I'm learning rather than what I'm doing."

"Works for me," I said.

Andrea dropped into her seat and nodded her head toward Rachel. "She and I have had this coaching session before. And she's right: When I see Roberto in degrees of weakness, I lose control. My emotions get the best of me, which I've learned means I forfeit my ability to lead . . . as I so effectively demonstrated for you just a moment ago."

I was struck by the contrast in this person in front of me. Her brutal honesty – with herself and how she sees the world – intrigued me. "You're quite candid," I said.

"The team has certainly been candid with me," Andrea chuckled and looked down at her desk. "My 360 survey was impressive, wasn't it, Rachel?"

"Why don't you share what you discovered," Rachel said.

"I believe the words were, 'I dismantle people's ability to respond,'" she said. "That's one of the two pieces of feedback that stung the most."

"I bet it would. Why did it sting, in particular?" I asked.

"Because I'm in a position of responsibility, that's why. How can I lead if I'm dismantling another person's ability to respond?" Andrea asked. "Leaders are supposed to develop others' capability to respond, not crush it."

"Where are you making progress in this area that you feel good about?" Rachel asked.

Andrea considered this for a moment and said, "I'm embarrassed to say." We all sat quietly, and I began to think of a different question to ask. Then Andrea showed her courage. "I've always wanted people to succeed," she said. "And I know I need them to succeed if I'm going to succeed. Sometimes, though, I get so attached to what I want us to get done that it becomes torture for me when I don't see us making the progress I want. It wells up, and pretty soon, all these thoughts bombard my mind: Why are these people so stupid? Why am I stuck with so many incompetent people!"

"Andrea," Rachel said with her eyebrows lifted, "help me understand how that's evidence of making progress as a leader."

"Because I feel like I'm becoming more aware. Before, I never even realized the damage I was creating by seeing people in degrees of stupidness and utter incompetence," she said. "I realize it seems simple, but I'm here to tell you, I'm now aware I have to make this change."

A buzzing tone interrupted the conversation, and Rachel looked down at her phone. "I've got to go. Please, continue the conversation without me. I think it's going somewhere important." At the door, Rachel looked back at me and asked, "Stop by my office when you're done?"

I nodded, and Rachel closed the door behind her. I pivoted in my chair and smiled at Andrea. "Where does she think this is going?" I asked.

"She probably wants to know if I'm talking about Roberto," she said. I sat quietly. Her interpretation of Rachel's intentions was important. "And I am," she said as she put her elbows on her desk. Then, after looking at the closed door a second time, she said, "Off the record, I must confess: Most of the time I despise Roberto. How this guy got to the level we're at is beyond me."

"What does he do that triggers you?" I said.

"He acts like a know-it-all! He finishes your sentences. He always has a better idea than you. He does things on his watch. He's always positioning himself. He thinks his function is flawless and our organizational troubles are caused by everyone else." She took a short breath. "And I know he's always ruining my name behind my back every chance he gets!"

There was little doubt this person in front of me was hurting. And with a Degrees of Strength application, it was easy to decipher something important: She cares about the success of the organization. "So, what do you do with all that?" I asked.

"What do you mean?" she asked, sounding a bit exasperated. "What do I do with all *what*?"

"Just that," I said. "What do you do with that focus, that mindset?"

"Agghh!" Andrea put her hands up and slouched in her chair. "Stop. Stop. Give me a moment."

Caught off guard by her abruptness, I sat back.

"There were two pieces of feedback from my 360 that stung." She paced herself. "They told me I am 'impossible to communicate with because I act like a know-it-all.'" She visibly seized up and through pursed lips said, "So how's that for building your confidence? They're saying I am to them . . . what Roberto is to me."

I opened my mouth but was stopped when Andrea put her hand up.

"First, let's start with this: I'm not a know-it-all. In fact, I'm telling you I firmly believe that if a leader isn't learning, then the organization isn't growing. So, the logical question then becomes: *How* am I communicating that's giving people this false impression?

"This is how Degrees of Strength inspires, because the solution is right in front of me." She reached over and grabbed a card on the corner of her desk. "I wrote this down the moment I heard it:

> *When you see others in degrees of weakness, you diminish them and their potential. Therefore, you do not feel the need to reach out to them or to engage them. Rather, you talk 'to' or 'at' them – at best – or 'down to them' – at worst."*

She looked up at me. "Painful, isn't it?"

"Have you ever considered writing a card with a focus of Degrees of Strength?" I asked. "A focus on what you want rather than what you don't want?"

Andrea tilted her head as she examined the idea. "I never thought of that," she said, reclining in her chair. "If I did . . ." she gazed up at the ceiling, ". . . it would sound like this:

> *When you see others in Degrees of Strength, you expand their greatness and seize their potential."*

She paused and then finished,

> *"Therefore, you are compelled to reach out to them and engage them. You talk 'with' them, and in partnership discover a better path forward."*

She wrote down her new quote and put down her pen.

"Andrea, what drives you crazy about that?" I said, making certain she knew it was a jest.

She smiled and brought herself forward in her chair. "Thanks. Thinking has always been my strong suit. *Doing* remains my opportunity."

"I have to commend you, Andrea. You are giving yourself to this process. And, from my perspective, you are much stronger than the average person. I think a lot of people would shut down if they received the feedback you've gotten. By acknowledging that you're not perfect and seeing the opportunities in front of you, you are giving yourself a unique advantage."

"That's new for me," she said, nodding her head. "Intellectually, I've understood that being vulnerable makes you a better leader. But until

Degrees of Strength, I haven't been able to model that approach. And, as Rachel made clear, the perfection game was killing me."

"I recognize that game," I said and paused. I wanted Andrea to know that the challenges she was wrestling with were normal. "I think a lot of us as leaders hold a vision for what we want done – and the fatal error comes when we *expect* others to act a certain way versus *accept* what happens along the way. It took me a while to realize that by expecting – or demanding – people be and do certain things, I was grossly limiting our potential to one vision: mine. But when I quit fighting the reality that we're not perfect, and I included their vision on how to move forward, suddenly, the quantity and quality of ideas skyrocketed. And our mistakes became valuable resources in our efforts to improve." I grinned at Andrea. "I wish I could sit here and tell you I was perfect with this technique, but that would be *expecting* the unachievable."

We both chuckled. "What else did Rachel tell you?" I asked.

"The day before we started this process she told me, 'Andrea, I believe in you. Your strengths are significant, and you can help us get where we need to go. But you've got to change specific behaviors if you want to be on this team moving forward.'

"I was shocked," Andrea said with her eyes wide open. "She just laid it on the line. 'You're playing a perfection game. You measure everything and everyone backward from where or what you perceive as the standard of perfection. But perfection is not a destination, it's a concept. Therefore, perfection is illusive because it is a personal perspective.'

"She told me, 'We're about to launch a new methodology, an improved way of living and leading. If you want to be in the role you're in, you need to help us model this approach. It's called Degrees of Strength, and the first thing I need you to show greater mastery in is this: Instead of slowing us down with a relentless focus on where we're not perfect – you need to accelerate us by further developing our excellence.'"

Andrea shifted in her seat and continued. "I wouldn't say that was my moment of acceleration. But I got the message. I love my job. I want to be here, so I appreciate that Rachel was direct with me . . ."

"What difference did it make?" I asked.

"Rachel shoots straight. Yet, I can feel her fighting for me. She wants me to succeed."

"She does appear to be able to balance those two approaches," I said. "It's so easy to go overboard on being direct without the support."

"It's a terrific combination: direct and honest feedback – combined with a determination to ensure I improve. I know she's got my back," Andrea answered. "If I contrast that with my own leadership, I think I have the direct feedback part mastered. But I create no inspiration to –" she stopped. "But I need to create even more inspiration for others."

I smiled as a way of acknowledging how her paradigm and words shifted to Degrees of Strength.

"My mantra has always been 'I tell it like I see it,'" Andrea said with an air of irony. "It was part of my wake-up call when Rachel asked me, 'Why is it that every time you 'tell it like you see it,' people walk away confused and upset, partnerships are dismantled, and performance drops?'

"I wanted to answer by saying, 'This is who I am. Take it or leave it.' But I knew that if I did, she'd leave me behind."

It was clear to me that Andrea realized her old method is not biased for growth. Leaders can force people to adapt to their style, but it's better to facilitate a mutual style *with* those you're leading. When you see them in Degrees of Strength, the common ground becomes obvious.

I looked at her and wondered if she would make one more stretch: "Have you been able to do that with Roberto?"

"You like asking the tough questions, don't you?" she said. "No, I haven't – wait." She put her finger up and interrupted herself. "If I use the Degrees of Strength technique . . . the truth is, I have done this with him. The degrees to which I have succeeded are small – far from perfection. But the progress is there."

"I have to ask the obvious – and important – question," I said. "How are you making this incremental progress?"

"I liked the story the facilitator told in the session, the one about the race of the parked cars."

"That is a popular one," I said, without seeing how it would relate to her work with Roberto. "Tell it to me from your perspective."

She stood up and pointed out the window at the parking lot, then said, "Imagine your team is entered into a contest every day it shows up for work:

The first team to push its car to the other end of the parking lot – wins! Your team has to choose one of three cars to get behind and push: Car #1 is rolling forward; #2 is sitting motionless; and car #3 is rolling backward.

"Logical people would want their team to get behind the car that is rolling forward. Yet, if you were to follow me and listen to the words I use all day, you'd hear how those words diminish momentum, slow things down, and make work more difficult," she said. Her frustration was palpable. "I'm as serious about winning as anybody here – yet my approach is illogical!"

She picked up her Degrees of Strength card and said, "I've been using classic and common degrees of weakness language. I talk about our progress – I talk about people – as if it's possible to have less than zero.

'We never . . . they can't . . . he always . . . our problems . . . they won't . . . .' This language shapes a mindset, a belief that my team has to operate from." She put her hands up. "Every day they come to work and have to get behind the car that's rolling backward. No wonder they feel as though I dismantle their ability to respond."

She threw down the card in resignation. And that's when I realized how hard she was working on this. Any day now she would make the connection. She was in the midst of her moment of acceleration.

"Obviously, you're still here. Rachel must see progress," I said.

Andrea took a deep breath. "Yes. She does. She finds the perfect time to tell me where I'm making the progress – and the difference it is making. I've got to tell you, that feedback is my lifeline."

The acceleration moment, as they call it, is a transformation. It's the transition from mere intelligence to applied wisdom. It's what Rachel experienced in talking with her husband's uncle. If I could tell Andrea one thing, I would tell her it's not mechanical. It's outside the realm of logic, in some ways, because it begins with looking at things differently, from a different paradigm. It's about you and your relationship with yourself in the context of how you see your world.

If I asked the right question, I might be able to assist her. But at the risk of creating a distracting focus, I stayed quiet, trusting she would lead herself there.

"The person I need to see in Degrees of Strength is *me*. It's come to that. And now I'm convinced that until I do, how can I possibly see others in Degrees of Strength?

"But, you know me," Andrea said rolling her eyes. "I'm bent on being perfect, so I'm constantly measuring *backward* from the bar of perfection . . . what I'm not doing right . . . where I keep making mistakes. This sustained mindset does nothing but frustrate me. In turn, it means I frustrate others.

"So, I really have begun to listen for those little moments when Rachel tells me, 'This is the progress I'm most pleased with . . .' or 'Here's where you are moving us forward . . .' or 'Here's an important difference you're making . . .' These types of comments immediately recalibrate me and set me on the path of leveraging the Degrees of Strength that exist."

Over the years, it's become clear that people reach and move through their moment of acceleration differently. Andrea has probably had to work at it harder than most. Being here to support her in becoming a greater contributor to the team and the company – and a better person for herself – is like witnessing a high-voltage event. But now we had to complete the process so she could demonstrate this ability, repeatedly, on her own.

"I get that it all starts with you," I said. "I'd like to go back to the classic degrees of weakness language you said you were using – the language that's the equivalent of putting your team behind a car that's rolling backward. More specifically, what does it sound like day to day?"

"Besides the obvious blanket statements such as 'Nobody ever . . .' or 'Everyone is . . . ,' there are more subtle ways." Andrea put her fingers up and ticked them off: our sales are a disaster, we're not listening to our customers, we never execute efficiently, there's no accountability here, we don't have the resources, and . . ." She stopped. "Do you want me to continue? I can."

She leaned forward. "This is all coded language for *we can't*. It is pure degrees of weakness. This language creates momentum backward. It implies and communicates that there's nothing to work from, nothing to build upon. This, of course, is an illusion because there's always something to leverage. This is how Rachel, who I think is an Accelerator, as you call them, differentiates herself: She tells the truth – and does it in a way that generates even more momentum. She puts us with the car that is already rolling forward."

"Would you consider yourself an Accelerator?" I asked.

She smiled. "That's a trick question. I'm smart."

"Yes. But what's the answer?"

"Of course I am. We all are – but to varying degrees. Because Rachel's fighting for me, I'm committed to becoming a more capable Accelerator so I can contribute more," she said.

"You stated 'coded' language. What is coded language for Degrees of Strength?"

"That's easy," she said. "Well, easy to understand – not easy for me to apply. Yet."

This is the beautiful thing about an acceleration moment like Andrea's. She had made it, and she was reaping the rewards of her dedicated self-work. Yet she wasn't fully aware that she had important momentum. When Rachel saw her next, she would appear unlike she had in the past.

"Essentially, coded language of Degrees of Strength would be any communication that points out that what you desire already exists." She put her hand up again. "The obvious Degrees of Strength words are: more of, in addition to, better, next, increase, or further. Some examples of those words in action:

- What can we do more of to improve sales quickly?
- In addition to what we know, what else are our customers telling us?
- What's the next and immediate thing we can do to execute more efficiently?
- How do we increase accountability?
- How do we better leverage the resources we have?"

"That's a great list. You obviously have been doing more than listening," I said.

Andrea shook her head. "Those Degrees of Strength questions roll off my tongue as if I'm an expert. Intellectually, I can do it. But when I'm in an argument with Roberto, the twelve inches between my head and my heart can sometimes prove to be a long distance. Memorizing Degrees of Strength language isn't going to get me where I know I can go. Internalizing this approach is what's necessary."

I watched Andrea to see if she wanted to continue that thought. With the extended silence, I decided to acknowledge her for the aptitude she was displaying with several tools. "I noticed that all of the examples you gave of Degrees of Strength language came in the form of questions. If those are the types of questions you're asking, it tells me your team isn't getting a simple cheerleader approach."

"You don't take me for the cheerleader type do you?" she smiled. "Discovering *how* you shift your focus from degrees of weakness to Degrees of Strength was just as important to me as knowing what this tool is. The 3 Mind Factors assist me in understanding that fact. Because I go in the direction of my focus, whatever I am focused on becomes key," she said. "And nothing – nothing – changes a person's focus like questions. And so, when I ask Forward Focus Questions, I can immediately move myself and others to a greater Degrees of Strength paradigm.

"There's something more about Forward Focus Questions that compels me to use them. Rachel and I talked about this: It's my ticket to developing more responsibility in others. The fact that people say I'm 'dismantling' their effectiveness is a clear message that they actually *want* to be great. They want the responsibility. They want to do well. And so, if I can ask – excuse me – *when* I ask Forward Focus Questions, I'm acknowledging this fact. I'm communicating that I know they want – and can be – responsible.

And I'm further activating their ability to do so."

I had to write down a few of these points. When I finished the note and looked up, Rachel was staring at me, ready to speak.

"Did you talk to anyone in HR yet?"

"No," I answered. "Should I?"

Andrea shook her head. "No. I'll save you the time. They've been talking to me about a high-potential employee we just lost."

I wanted to hear the story, so I kept my mouth shut.

"I wrestle – I mean, I really struggle – with the idea that if we are not telling people how poorly we're performing, we're not telling the truth. I want to run around here and shout, 'People! Wake up! Things are bad! Things are *really* bad!'"

Andrea took a deep breath. "After one particular meeting, this guy, Brett, who's basically a new hire, of all things, asked to speak with me. We stepped aside, and he had the guts to ask me, 'How much longer are things going to be bad?'

"I'm thinking to myself, 'This kid has a lot of nerve.' I looked at him so he knew it was a dumb question and said, 'Until we get our act together.'
"He looked right back at me and said, 'Well, Andrea, this company hired me because it thought I had my act together. The first time you told us how badly we were doing, I raised my effort a notch. The second and third and fourth time you told us? Now I just say screw it. That's why I'm here to see you. There are a lot of people down there who have quit – they just haven't

told you. I decided to come up here and tell you.'"

"So he left?" I asked.

"Yes. And that kills me. I wasn't capable of creating an environment that would keep this kid here. And if what he said is true, those who are still here aren't *really* here."

"That's the number one performance issue in most companies – a disengaged workforce," I said. "Yet I don't think leaders are showing the level of leadership responsibility you're demonstrating, Andrea."

"It was all about my management style. It finally stung enough that I understood what Rachel and everyone else was talking about."

"What's that?" I asked.

"I was so afraid that if we didn't talk about how bad things were we would be lying. But this approach is not about lying. The Degrees of Strength technique doesn't mean we don't tell the truth or don't state our perspective of where we believe things currently stand. Degrees of Strength is about telling that truth or perspective in a way that releases us to move forward faster. This is about communicating in a way that gets us to resolution quicker."

I leaned forward and was about to congratulate her on the significance of what she was sharing. She waved me off.

"I know. You want to hear what that sounds like," she said. "It's like this:

- 'It's essential that we address these results and see immediate improvement.'

- Or 'The current results are not acceptable. We must improve immediately.'
- Or 'It's critical that our customers experience our best-in-class effort. What will we do right now to ensure that happens?'

Or..." Andrea stopped. "I could go on, but it's important we address what's really happening with these words."

She cleared her throat and continued. "Rachel models this clearly as she uses the Degrees of Strength technique: This is not about lowering standards or expectations. There are still consequences if people are not performing at acceptable levels. She's doing that with me. She's made it very clear what sort of mindset – what sort of culture – I need to model if I want to stay on this team."

Andrea stopped for a moment and then finished her thought. "But with Degrees of Strength, you enable people to perform to the level of expectation. And . . ." she paused. "Frankly, you create a fertile opportunity for people to go beyond expectations. Because that's what I intend to do."

I smiled and said, "You're a bit of an enigma, Andrea. I walked in here and experienced you as a bit intimidating. And now, here you are – dare I say – inspiring me."

She returned my smile. "Don't I wish you could have participated in my 360 survey!"

We laughed and I asked, "But Andrea, if I can feel that way around you, surely others do."

"No. I've got to own the experience others are having around me and the results we've been delivering. I've been anything but inspiring," she said. "But you helped me realize something. I've always complained about the fact that we don't have many inspired leaders around here. Perhaps I've been missing the fundamental ingredient: To be inspiring to others, *I* must be inspired. When I am inspired, then I become inspiring to others. When others become inspired, they become inspiring to yet more people."

"What's your ticket to being inspired, Andrea?"

"Isn't it the same for each of us? It's a function of being able to see what's possible – and to believe in what's possible. And it goes back to what we talked about, the primary way to shift the focus to what's possible is Forward Focus Questions. When we ask these types of questions, we are communicating in the language of the possibilities – a future we can create."

I didn't know what to say in response to what Andrea had just shared. I wondered if Rachel knew that Andrea was so close to an acceleration moment – and that's why she wanted us to spend this time together. Andrea had made a remarkable shift right in front of me. And she knew it, too.

"When I agreed to this time with you, I thought I was doing a favor for Rachel," Andrea said with a chuckle. "Now I can see that Rachel was simply leading again. She must have known that by discussing this topic, something important would happen."

"What has happened that's important to you?" I asked.

"I've finally answered my question," she said. "The question that's been driving me crazy: Why aren't people more responsible? The answer is that I have not been as responsible as I should be as a leader. By using a degrees of weakness approach, I've been communicating to people 'you're not good enough.' And how would anyone respond to such a consistent message?"

"I'd stop working as hard – or quit altogether," I answered.

"When you do that, you provide me with the evidence I'm looking for – that you're not responsible. And the destructive cycle deepens. I send more degrees of weakness messages, and you quit more."

"It's a lose-lose formula," I said.

She picked up her pen, wrote something down, and then looked up at me. "My leadership determines whether people are response-*able* or not."

We both stood up and began to walk toward the door. Andrea spoke first. "Let's keep this conversation between us for now. Okay?"

I nodded and said, "But I'm curious. Are you ready to talk about this with Roberto?"

Andrea stopped and thought about this for a moment, then said, "No. Not yet. This isn't easy. There's no elixir. Rachel is at the level she's at in her thinking – in her leadership – because she's been working with this for a while. She makes it sound as though the acceleration moment was a flash of instant transformation. And it may work that way for some. But she told me that she was beginning to think, to *feel*, this way years before she ever talked to her husband's uncle. The Degrees of Strength technique simply captured what she was trying to say and how she was trying to lead. But it's different for me. I've just begun to get over myself and begin the process of discovery."

"If it's not easy, what keeps you going?" I asked.

"I have thought about that, and I can tell you: I'm sick of the misery. I'm sick of the pain and frustration that mounts every day when I use the degrees of weakness approach. For my entire life, I've believed that there's got to be a better way. There just has to be. And here comes Rachel, cruising around in her wheelchair, *leading*. And I think to myself, 'Are you kidding me?' Who am I to be miserable?"

Andrea shook her head. "I'm going to get philosophical on you for a moment." She looked back at her desk and then right at me. "I truly believe we're supposed to be enjoying all of this. All this work. All this effort. It's not supposed to be a grind. It's not supposed to destroy us. It's supposed to enrich us.

"And, frankly, it haunts me to think about being on my deathbed some day and in that moment, when I ask myself, 'Did I succeed?' Good heavens. I have to be able to answer 'yes' to that question. I just have to."

I stood silently for a moment. And then smiled. "Thank you, Andrea."

As I moved to the door, Andrea said, "One more thing. What you're talking about – all these questions you're asking – you shouldn't look at this as a device to drive leadership change. It's a life change . . . that affects your leadership."

I nodded. "Got it."

CHAPTER SIX

Case Study: The Generator of Trust

Andrea reminds us that we can make communication more difficult than it needs to be. The Degrees of Strength technique makes communication easier. We minimize hidden motivations because the agenda is clear: We can all win at this. I believe in you and our work together. I know we can move forward.

The approach and language of Degrees of Strength naturally develops one of the most prized elements of any team's acceleration equation: trust. Without trust, a team cannibalizes itself, attacking and destroying the strengths in each other – the very thing needed for survival. Without trust, the team is left with a link that is no stronger than a child's handmade paper chain. This is no match against the currents of the swift-moving market.

When team members focus on and reinforce the strengths in their peers, regardless of how small those strengths are, every interaction becomes a bonding mechanism. Now, "weaknesses" become nonexistent. Therefore, every interaction feeds and strengthens the partnership. The trust that evolves between people and business functions is as strong as titanium chain links and is resilient against the unpredictable forces of the market.

"It's actually illogical," says a client of ours who works for one of the most respected consulting companies in the world. "You can't create stronger trust by functioning with an 'I-don't-trust-you' focus. If you see your trust with a customer or partner in degrees of weakness, because you go toward your focus, you can only create *less* trust. And who wants to be a part of that?"

Accelerators are trust generators. This leader's team is responsible for implementing broad-scale software changes for its customers. "The Degrees of Strength approach has transformed our performance. The partnerships that we have formed with our customers are noticeably different. Instead of going in and being the 'experts,' we are accelerating results by taking a trust-based partnership approach."

You may be familiar with the typical approach to creating partnerships. (It's a paradox that plagues slow teams.) Someone, be it a customer, a teammate, or the head of another function, does something "wrong" and – bam! – the degrees of weakness person says, "I don't trust that person anymore." As if that's not bad enough, the degrees of weakness person accelerates the reverse momentum by moving to a "now-you-have-to-earn-my-trust-back" mindset. In that moment, the organization's dismal fate has been sealed.

Those who understand that you go in the direction of your focus, the third of the 3 Mind Factors, know it will be impossible to build trust. To the extent the focus is on where there is no trust, there will be no trust.

Accelerators work differently as they serve their customers. They leverage the Degrees of Strength as they use these five important steps to form trust-based partnerships:

1. Demonstrate the mindset that the customer's current system or approach needs development – but the customer isn't broken.
2. Understand and build upon what's already working, thereby saving resources and building a sense of forward momentum early.
3. Ask for and utilize the customer's ideas, thus leveraging the inherent wisdom already in place.
4. Provide ample focus on and give feedback that provides clarity of the performance that's needed for success.
5. Add to momentum along the way by celebrating the small victories, thereby generating more confidence and momentum throughout the project.

"We know from experience that a degrees of weakness approach corrodes trust in every interaction. With Degrees of Strength, trust becomes a natural byproduct. And everyone wins," says this leader. And her team consistently experiences the difference in this evolved approach. Most importantly, the team's customers report the striking difference: It's why the team is often responsible for efforts that clients consider to be the "best ever."

CHAPTER SEVEN

CHAPTER SEVEN
Eric and Luc: Transforming Performance

"Come in," said the voice on the other side of the door.
It was Rachel. As I walked into her office, she and a gentleman I didn't recognize both looked up. "Welcome back! And please, join us." She spun herself over to a conference table and motioned to the man next to her. "I'd like you to meet Eric. He's from finance."

Eric and I shook hands, and as we sat down, there was a loud rapping at the door. Rachel looked at her watch and said, "Just like clockwork." She looked toward the door. "Come in!"

The man who entered had an oversized grin that dominated his small face. With a quicker pace than you'd expect for the size of his light-framed body, he was in front of me in an instant. "Hello. Luc's my name. R&D," he said. We greeted one another, and then he turned to Eric. "And you, my friend! The crazy American, Rachel, has allowed the German and the French in the same room once again!" The two men laughed and gave each other a polite hug, and we all sat.

"I saw Andrea in the hallway," said Luc, "and she looks like she just returned from a spa. She was so relaxed, so pleasant."

"What happened to her?" Eric asked.

"She spent time with him," Luc said, tipping his head toward me, "reviewing our progress since the sessions."

"Oh. I wasn't sure," Eric said.

"Luc is right, Eric," Rachel said. "You two have done an extraordinary job in the organization redefining how we generate greater performance. We wouldn't be where we're at if it weren't for you – so it is important that you have a voice during our friend's visit."

"Specifically, what this trip has evolved into is how people are accelerating performance by using the Degrees of Strength technique. I'd like to know your perspective and experience with this," I said.

"Performance!" Luc said. "My favorite topic. And you've got the right man here for answers," he said, patting Eric on the back. "Repeat what you told me six months ago when we had our acceleration moment."

Eric looked at his colleague with a question mark on his face. "You mean about the value of a leader?"

"Yes. Yes. The value of leadership, Eric," Luc said, sitting back.

Eric shrugged his shoulders. "I said too many leaders are corrupt with an inflated sense of the value they bring to an organization. Where they sit, they can see things those they are leading can't see. But they mistakenly believe that because they can see such things that they're smarter than everyone else. This creates difficulties for them that they don't even realize, because the fact remains: Their effectiveness as a leader is only as effective as the message received by those they're leading. If a job is going to get done, we can't stop with the vision and expectations established by the leader – it's what those we are leading *think* that determines performance."

Eric casually shifted in his seat and continued. "Six months ago we were full of ourselves. That's why our performance was so poor. We thought we had all the answers. We were blind to the understanding that high performance is contingent upon the fact that those doing the work in our organization must have the answers."

"He's brilliant, yes?" Luc said with a smile. "And let me tell you, just six short months ago, that German sitting there wouldn't have said anything like that." Luc leaned forward and finished in a mock whisper, "You know those Germans. They get so impatient with how slow the rest of us think."

"Luc!" Rachel said.

"No. No," Eric said. "Allow him his fun. Only the French know how to manipulate the conversation for their benefit."

The three of them burst into laughter, led by the loudest, Luc. The tiny man then put his hands up and said, "Seriously. This is what I'm talking about: In the past, our differences broke us. Now, with Degrees of Strength, our differences are our alchemy, the accelerator, that produces a bond. This gives us an advantage over our competition."

"That resonates strongly," I said.

"In effect, it gives us the ability to deliver on our collective potential," Luc said. "If you seek extraordinary performance, if you seek performances from others that are beyond what you can deliver yourself, then you must release them from the constraints of your vision. You must lead them – and create a culture around them – that allows them to discover a greater expression of themselves that is consistent with the values and mission of the organization."

"That was difficult for me to understand at first," Eric said. "What did this mean, 'greater expression'? Frankly, it sounded too emotional for me. But then, once when I was having coffee with my brother, I noticed something. He is an engineer who designs the finest motors in the automobile industry. He seemed to be glowing as he was talking about his work. I saw something very compelling in my brother: As he talked about his job, he did so as if the effort he provides each day isn't really work at all. It's something else.

"So I decided to conduct an experiment. I asked him, 'What don't you like about your work?' He thought about that for a moment. After a bit, he mentioned the paperwork he had to do. 'It is wicked,' he said. I asked, 'What else?' He thought some more and he said, 'There are two people on our team who are worthless. When I get stuck on a project with them, it is the end of me.'"

Eric paused long enough that Luc jumped in, "And what happened?"

"Directly in front of me," Eric answered, "my brother transformed from someone who was inspired about his work . . . to someone who wasn't excited about his job. Because of his focus, because I had asked him backward-focus questions, I dismantled his inspiration."

"Oh, you are the evil one," Luc said.

"Certainly, I didn't end the experiment there. If this Degrees of Strength technique is legitimate, it means that there are strengths in *all* areas. I wanted to test that.

"I asked my brother if he'd be willing to try something with me regarding what he had just shared. He agreed. I asked him, 'It's clear you love the element of precision in your work. What is it about this paperwork, that you said you don't like, that is necessary for you to deliver excellence in your work?'

"He thought about that for a moment. I figured he was going to answer with his typical, 'Nothing.' But you could tell he wanted to move forward, too. Finally, he said, 'It helps us do two things: one, track our progress, which means we can measure against our standards. And two, it allows us to communicate with one another in a way where there's no gray. Everything is clear.'

"At this point," Eric continued, "I was just about to ask him another Forward Focus Question when he put his hand up and said, 'For example, just one month ago, we caught what we thought was an error in our paperwork, but in reality, it wasn't a data-entry error, it was flaw in the approach to the system we were using.'

"My brother continued to tell this story about what they discovered. And as the story unfolded, I watched him become 'high' on his job again. It was remarkable. Right in front of me, we had taken what was originally a weakness – and transformed it by identifying and focusing on the inherent strengths."

"When you did that, you transformed your brother," Luc added. "But what about the two peers he dislikes?"

"Yes, that was next. The experiment continued when I asked my brother, 'If the two people on your team who challenge you were gone tomorrow, what qualities would you miss the most?'

"My brother immediately laughed and said, 'That would be a dream! If only they could be gone tomorrow.' But my brother is emotionally intelligent and knew it was an important question."

"That's an important point: emotional intelligence," Luc interrupted. "I see too many people spend most of their day fantasizing that the circumstances in their life be different than they are currently. Instead of being responsible and saying, 'This is our current situation. How do we best move forward?' they spend enormous amounts of time wishing things were different or those they despise weren't on their team. And that's not even reality!"

"Luc, please," Rachel said with mock exacerbation. "Let Eric finish."

"Ah, yes!" Luc said. "Your brother. The experiment. Eric, it's not like you Germans to get distracted. Please. Continue."

Eric smiled at Luc, who returned the grin and then continued. "After some thought, my brother said, 'They both are highly trained. One has more experience with our type of engine than I'll ever have. And the other has some sort of sixth sense that allows him to troubleshoot with remarkable speed.'

"'If you didn't have those qualities, what would the team have to do to deliver the precision necessary to succeed?' I asked him. He replied

somewhat reluctantly, 'I'm not actually sure. We would have a hole to fill.'"
Eric sat up in his chair and added, "I could feel a foundation for
momentum begin to build for my brother, so I asked the next Forward
Focus Question. 'What is your responsibility in developing a stronger
partnership with these two?' He looked at me in near shock. '*My*
responsibility?' I said, 'Yes. You have two choices: Be a victim of the
differences between you and them or be accountable to your values and
the team and lead forward.'

"My brother had to think on this for some time. Finally he said, 'In all
honesty, I probably need to stop speaking poorly about them. These guys
probably know I don't like them. But they have to start respecting me, too.'

"Hearing my brother say that gave me a tremendous insight: Until then,
my level of responsibility to act and lead more effectively with my own
team was contingent on other people acting responsible first. Just like my
brother, I want others to respect me before I start respecting them. Now
I could see it clearly: My brother would stay stuck, mired at that point in
his career development, if he kept using this approach.

"When I shared with my brother what he had just taught me, he sat up in
his chair and said, 'That's what brothers are for.' He felt smart. I didn't care
that it was actually his lesson that had become my lesson, I wanted him to
have the credit – I wanted him to feel good about it."

"Why?" Luc asked.

"Because now he is more likely to change his behavior. It is his idea, not
mine," Eric answered.

"Did he change?" Rachel asked.

"I will have to follow up and see what sort of progress he's making," Eric answered. "But at that point, my experiment was complete, and the findings were clear: 1) My brother, when in an inspired state, didn't feel like his job was work; 2) When he focused on what he didn't like, he lost his inspiration; 3) By addressing those same factors in Degrees of Strength, he saw the opportunity and took responsibility; and 4) He could now move forward with those same factors present and remain inspired, regardless of the circumstances."

"Yes," Luc sat forward, eager to contribute. "Eric's experiment highlights a key difference between the Degrees of Strength technique and the paradigm many people function from."

"What paradigm is that?" Rachel asked.

"Increasingly, I hear people say 'focus on your strengths,'" Luc said. "But this implies, of course, that you also have *weaknesses*. This has driven me crazy for years! In an effort to improve someone's performance, I was instructed to only focus on that person's strengths. But what happens if the discipline in which an individual is weak, say, strategic thinking, is an area in which we desperately need to deliver value to the customer? Am I supposed to ignore a person's inability to think strategically because this is not an area of strength?"

"There are probably a lot of good managers who have lost their job with such an approach," Eric added.

"Precisely," said Luc. "But it gets worse if I use that thinking. In order to save my job, I decide to focus on that person's weaknesses anyhow. Now I have two options: 1) I can say he or she is a poor performer in the area of strategic thinking . . . which, of course, disenfranchises this individual. Who likes to hear over and over that they are not good at doing something? Or 2) I can blow smoke and set up mirrors and try to falsely convince the person that he or she is good at strategic thinking. I don't care if you're French or American or German or from Mars, no true leader enjoys option 2."

"Which leaves us with option 1," Eric said. "And that, I am learning, is disheartening."

"Which is the beauty of the Degrees of Strength technique," Luc said. "It gives you a third option. It is a step beyond the 'focus on the areas of your strengths,' because everyone has some level of strength in every area. So I can go to this person who in the past has suffered with strategic thinking and begin to focus and expand those areas in which there is already some proficiency in strategic thinking."

"For clarity, I'd like to add something I struggled with early on," Rachel said. "And I'll ask you two to ensure the rest of this team understands this: By using the Degrees of Strength approach, we are not proposing we put people in areas where they have fewer strengths – unless we intentionally want to develop and make those strengths greater. We all know we'll get greater performance when people are playing in the areas of their greatest strengths."

"I agree," Luc said. "There are various and effective ways to improve the performance of a team, such as putting people in a position where they can succeed. We should add other variables, such as ensuring clear objectives and a plan of execution are created, two-way information flow exists, resource management is effective, and collaboration is present." Luc leaned forward. "But those were all things that Rachel's predecessor was focused on, and we were still delivering mediocre scores."

He turned and faced Rachel, "You differentiated yourself by adding the human factor to this list of performance variables. You knew that to transform our performance, you had to change our behaviors. And to do that, you discovered you had to change our paradigm, the way we were seeing ourselves, each other, and the work we do."

"She accomplished that by shifting our thinking from degrees of weakness to Degrees of Strength," Eric added.

"This has returned something quite valuable to me – something I cherish," Luc said. With an expression I hadn't yet seen on his face, Luc stated, "She has brought back my 'first-day freshness.'"

"What do you mean by that, my French friend," Eric said with one of his few smiles and a faux-French accent.

"When I walk into a bakery and it is full of freshly baked bread – oh! The delight for me! It transforms my senses," Luc said, kissing the air. "It is the same for us as humans. When I first walked into this company twenty-seven years ago, I felt that way. My first day, I felt as though I could – and would – do anything. I was so alive. I was so confident. I was so full of ideas.

"Then something began to happen. I didn't know it was occurring: As one day became the next, I quietly and gradually shifted to degrees of weakness.

When did it happen? When did I quit caring as much as I used to? When did I decide that the money I was making was more important than the experience I was having? Where did I learn that it was better to keep information from my peers for my personal gain? At what point did I start defining success by what my colleagues thought of me rather than what my children thought of me? When did I become okay with hiding from responsibility and avoiding risk? How did I get confused and falsely believe that it was better to see my teammate blamed for our failure than it was for me to stand up and say, 'I can.'" Luc shook his head slowly and finished. "In fact, when did I stop enjoying my reason for being here?"

The room was quiet for a moment. Then Luc added, "If Rachel hadn't introduced the Degrees of Strength technique to our operating system, I don't think I would have ever been aware of this erosion of virtues. But now, it's back. I'm back. And it feels like the first day I began working here. I have that first-day freshness."

"It's remarkable how quickly that experience, that mindset, returns," added Eric. "I remember when we first started working together. What was it, fifteen years ago?"

"Sixteen," Luc answered. "But who's counting. Your point is an important one."

Rachel lifted her arms. "You two! What's the point?"

Eric shrugged his shoulders again and nodded toward Luc. "We talked about it the other day. When we first started working together we were good friends. Even our families spent time together. But something happened. Somewhere along the way I began to see him in degrees of weakness, and as soon as that happened, our partnership evaporated and we stopped collaborating."

"That's the important point," Luc said, waving his finger. "When we saw each other and our ideas in Degrees of Strength, we could sit at the same table and collaborate. We could tell the truth about what we were thinking. And we may never have gotten to consensus, but it didn't matter. Excellence in performance doesn't require consensus. It requires collaboration and alignment."

"When we shifted to degrees of weakness, I didn't even want to be at the table with you," Eric said gently. "It took a lifetime to get anything done because we had to get to consensus in order to move forward."

"Why did you have to get to consensus?" I asked.

"Because after we left the room, no one trusted each other," Eric answered.

"How does Degrees of Strength allow you to collaborate more effectively?" I asked.

"Because everyone sees value – the elements of strength – in what each person is saying. We move from not just respecting diversity but soliciting it."

"It's more than that," Luc said. "When we see *ourselves* in Degrees of Strength, we are open to alternative opinions. Because I own my strengths, I don't have to get defensive or insecure if you offer a counter opinion. Therefore, I can be more responsible and say what I think needs to be said and say it in a way that invites more discussion rather than shutting people down."

"I'm glad you're bringing this up," Rachel said. "Luc, how does this apply to the performance issue we just heard about from our friends in product supply? What does it look like to apply what you're talking about with Mike?" Rachel looked over at me and added, "Mike's responsible for making sure our system runs like it was designed."

It was the first time in the conversation where Luc wasn't prepared to say something. After thinking, he said, "That's a very good question. I've been trying to find the best way to address the surprisingly low results.

"Mike is always harder on himself than I could ever be, and I trust that he already knows these scores are unacceptable. Still, I have to ensure we're aligned on the best path forward."

He looked at me. "This is where I used to ruin things. I was always an advocate for being direct with people, but *how* I was direct created a far worse mess. Degrees of Strength will allow me to confront this issue with Mike directly and in a way where Mike can move forward faster."

"Show me what that looks like," I said.

"Instead of fighting for greater results, I'm fighting for *his* success in delivering greater results. This means I'm not attacking him – I'm working with him to succeed in resolving the issue. Now, I can be even more candid and transparent.

"I'll look him in the eyes and start with a message on where we need to finish. I'll make sure I communicate why that is important. 'Mike, we must hit the process implementation target in the next quarter so the organization remains confident in our ability to deliver successfully.' I will then ask him questions to co-create the path forward. Because Mike is so hard on himself, I might start with a focus on where he already has momentum toward this target. For example, I might ask 'What strategic plans have the team been acting on that give you the confidence you can meet the objective?' and 'How will you adapt those plans with the team given the first-quarter performance?'"

"What happens if it's not a momentum issue?" Eric asked. "Our site managers gave me the indication that it's more of an execution issue. People aren't following through with what's been planned."

"That's a valuable insight," Luc said. He then turned to me and said, "Can you believe we once despised one another!" Luc let out his now-familiar, hearty laugh and said, "It sounds as though the execution issue is driven by breakdowns in accountability." He paused and thought for a moment. "To tell you the truth, the old me would immediately put the blame on Mike's team. If people aren't doing what they've been assigned, then we need to hold them accountable.

"But it's different for me now. It's taken me years to get there, but I now believe that if someone's not delivering on the objective, it's probably a leadership or systems issue. It could be the person has no ownership of the objective because he or she wasn't included in the design of the objective or the plan to achieve it."

"And the person wasn't buying what leadership was selling," added Eric.

"Exactly," said Luc. "If that were the case, after clearly stating that we must hit our implementation targets and why, I'd then coach Mike on asking his team questions such as:

- What does success look like in daily operations as your team delivers on target?
- What important benchmarks will be nonnegotiable moving forward?
- What additional actions do you need to take to ensure your team can be accountable to your deliverables?"

Luc tapped his thumb against his chin and continued. "But there's something else that could be affecting Mike's team. It's an issue that I'm noticing frequently in all our regions. We've got a lot of initiatives going all at once. I believe Mike's team could also be dealing with competing priorities and some initiative fatigue."

"You're reinforcing something I want to address in our next leadership team meeting," Rachel said. "I'm curious to know what questions you'll ask Mike because I could probably use them with our team."

"Sorry to sound redundant," Luc said, "but again, I would start out with what's important and why, and then we would co-discover the best path forward by breaking things down in achievable steps with questions such as:

- What are our top three priorities for delivering to our internal customer as we move into the new quarter?
- What is something we can take off our 'to-do' list to free some needed resources?
- What are two ways we can leverage resources and our efforts to increase efficiencies immediately?"

"My friend, you're getting good with those questions," Eric said with a small smile.

Luc nodded. "I'm at the point in my career –"

"No." Rachel interrupted him. "You're at a point in your awareness, not your career. If accelerating performance is only a function of time, we're in trouble. Because awareness largely drives performance – we can do something about that now."

"Okay. That's fair," Luc said. "My awareness is finally to the point that I'm done trying to motivate people. Mike's one of the best managers we've got. Either I believe in him or I don't. Because I've been focusing on his Degrees of Strength for the last six months, he knows I believe in him.

"The motivation he needs to improve the performance of his team resides in him. As a leader, it's my job to activate those motivations. If I were to rush in there and tell him what to do, this would reveal a degrees of weakness focus and send a message to him that 'I don't think you're capable.'" Luc shook his head and laughed.

"What's funny?" Eric asked.

"In the past, I sent degrees of weakness messages and *de*motivated people," said Luc. "I see now that they responded with defensiveness or stopped communicating, which is what most human beings would do."

"This means when you begin thinking everyone in the meeting is a problem," said Eric, "then you guarantee there's only one problem in the room."

"Your insights are important for us, and I ask you to reinforce the message to the rest of the organization, Luc," Rachel said. "Call it 'phase two' of our acceleration."

"What message specifically, Rachel?" Luc asked.

"That there's a big difference between the externally driven 'hold them accountable' approach and the internally developed 'ensure accountability' method. The first requires many more leadership resources and diminishes our long-term effectiveness. As I've said before, accountability is a personal choice. When we take the steps you're modeling for us and *ensure* accountability, individuals and teams can adapt much more effectively to unexpected events, which means we can move much quicker to and in the market."

"It puts the idea of 'continuous improvement' on steroids," Eric added.

When each interaction between every one of us moves from merely a transactional experience to a transformative one, improved performance is a natural byproduct."

"What does a transformational interaction look like to you," I asked.

"That's easy," Eric answered. "It's where the people involved know that the conversation, the interaction they're having, is – in that moment – the most important interaction in their day."

Luc leaned forward and said, "When you use every interaction to develop the person, your partnership with them, and the collective performance of the team, then we are not only continuously improving our product and how we make that product, we're improving our leadership and our culture . . . who we are as a company."

"Who we are as humans," Eric said.

There was a pause in the conversation, and both Luc and Eric looked at their cell phones. I got the message, and we all began moving toward the door. "I must confess," Rachel said. "This exercise has been good for me. It's helped me clarify how we can move forward even faster. And it's also reminded me of something."

We all stopped, and both Luc and Eric looked up from their phones. "What has it reminded you of?" Eric asked.

Rachel held the silence for a moment and then said, "It's reminded me of why I got into leadership in the first place."

CHAPTER EIGHT

Case Study: Agility, Agility, Agility

Every interaction of every day is an invitation to provide remarkable leadership. Leaders who use the Degrees of Strength approach when interacting with others see dramatic increases in performance as potential becomes reality. When Accelerators like Rachel empathetically interact with others and leverage the unique Degrees of Strength within a particular person, that teammate has greater freedom to achieve.

As this is accomplished, it naturally develops the capability of agility. Here's why: When employees are responsible or accountable to a boss (rather than something more important), they can't act or make decisions on their own. They will wait and make choices based upon their best guess of what the boss desires. Conversely, when people are responsible to themselves – their inner greatness – agility happens. In the most pressing moments, when facing the countless decisions that ultimately determine the success of the company, they make choices based upon: 1) Their values and the values of the organization; 2) What action is needed to serve in that moment; and 3) Their highest sense of what is right.

More than any time in history, agility is a requisite for success. Some bosses think this means they have to get faster at cascading information so others will do what they want done quicker. Savvy Accelerators know they must push decision making out of their office and empower those doing the work. They also know that agility is a skill to be learned and developed. This means equipping others with a technique to make better choices in the moments that fill up a day.

Ray is an Accelerator who models this approach. As the new VP of sales, he inherited a team that ranked last in sales for the second largest pharmaceutical company in the world. Ray reported, "It was obvious: Nothing short of a transformation would get us to where we needed to go."

Accelerating any change means challenges will occur as a natural function of growth and progress. Many bosses position these challenges as "problems," and thus begin the process of unwittingly putting their team into a perpetual state of crisis. Fire alarms sound and teams work feverishly to resolve each emergency. This approach subtly creates a belief that we are "not doing well" or "we're performing poorly" or "we're not capable or responsible." This crippling mindset is exhausting, debilitating, and eliminates any chance the team has of developing momentum – the antithesis of agility.

Ray took a different approach. As an Accelerator, he wanted his team members to differentiate themselves from their competition by how they respond to "problems." He did this by equipping people to make different choices, which allowed them to be more responsible and move faster.

Ray knew the challenges in front of his team were significant. Still, he held firm to his conviction that responsibility and accountability are personal choices. To transform results, he knew he had to alter how team members perceived the events and issues that filled their day.

"The prize for using Degrees of Strength, for being an Accelerator, means that instantly everything that happens during a day – good or bad – becomes an opportunity to do something special. It's remarkable to watch your team seize events that used to be 'problems,' find the Degrees of Strength that exist, and turn situations into moments of acceleration. By choosing to be responsible in such moments, we build the capability and capacity for speed and agility as we respond to and drive market conditions."

What happens when team members move from allowing daily events to define them . . . to growing in their ability to define events? The capacity to do this frees individuals and teams from the emotional wreckage that comes in the aftermath of when things go "wrong." Agility is the natural byproduct.

This skill of redefining how we see events means that life and business no longer happen to us; we happen to them.

"This notion of being an Accelerator changes you," said Ray. "If I've discovered anything in twenty-plus years in this business, change is a delicate subject. It's not something you can demand. You have to nurture it by changing how you approach it as a leader."

With his round face and a smile that immediately communicates he cares about you, Ray is a bulldog, relentless in his pursuit of high performance. "Everyone wants the year to go as planned," said Ray. "But life doesn't happen that way. If you think about it, 'problems' – moments of poor performance or results – are the most fertile ground for developing your team for success in the long term."

Ray has developed the capability in his team members to increasingly look at the tough issues they encounter through the Degrees of Strength lens – and then ask Forward Focus Questions:

- What's the critical issue here?
- What is already working in this area?
- Where do we have momentum – and how do we leverage that?
- What feedback are our customers giving us that we have to address immediately?
- How do we respond to customer feedback in a way that builds greater partnerships with them?
- What are three ways we can leverage our current resources even more?
- What are we learning about ourselves that will prove helpful in the long term?
- What could we have done earlier that would have created a better result in this situation?
- What are the successes taking place that we can celebrate and leverage?
- What does our collective responsibility look like moving forward?
- Who is stepping up and being responsible that we can identify as a model for the rest of the team?

Some bosses have to tell their team members they believe and have confidence in them. People who work for Accelerators can *feel* it. This means they're more likely to take responsibility, especially when things become difficult.

Ray knew that by developing his team's capability to respond to "problems" by asking Forward Focus Questions, the solutions would come quicker. And they did: Breakthrough ideas and initiatives, along with responsible execution, became the norm. New sales programs were developed, new product was successfully introduced to the market, and efforts to increase the frequency of contacts with customers all resulted in a transformation of results. Ray's team went from worst to first. In three years, it became the top sales team within the entire company, all brands and products being considered.

It gets better: Since the start of the "Great Recession" in 2008, the team grabbed seven points of share in an established market. Accordingly, Ray was recognized as one of the top organizational leaders at the world meetings, and the region has been recognized as "Country of the Year."

The casual observer might think, "Hey, give my team a new sales program, new product, and enhanced contacts with the customer and we can win, too." This is where Ray distinguishes himself again. "Many of those enhancements were a *result* of Degrees of Strength thinking," said Ray. "On top of that, how many times do you observe organizations that roll out new programs and expensive new initiatives and *still* get average results? It happens all the time. Products, strategies, and customers count – but how you *see and leverage* the products, strategies, and customers counts more."

One would think that this sort of success would be the pinnacle for Ray. However, it's now when Ray reveals the heart of an Accelerator. "The greatest reward for using Degrees of Strength is personal," Ray says. "I'm in control more. Day-to-day events rarely determine the quality of my experience anymore. This means I no longer have to wait until the weekend to enjoy my life."

When you meet Ray, you know in an instant he's not living a "throw-away" career. He has to make a difference for people. It's how he's programmed. You know as you interact with him that moving humanity forward is his purpose. "That's what's so inspiring for me. Leadership used to be all about making a profit. The discovery that with a tool like Degrees of Strength you can serve those you're leading, equip them for a greater life – and this ensures you deliver a *greater* profit – what's not transformational about that?

"With the tools of an Accelerator, I equip others to lead and create Accelerators around me. That's something that feeds on itself.

"This is when the magic happens: By developing others to be Accelerators, they then make a difference for those they come in contact with. Now our daily interactions begin to grow upon one another. Then, high performance isn't something we're trying to achieve, it's something we are.

"As a result, going to work feeds me. My job, and where I work, brings the best out of me. I'm surrounded by people I care about – and people who are as interested in my success as they are their own. When you think about that, how many people can say their culture at work makes them a better person?"

CHAPTER NINE

Rachel: What Leadership Can Be About

After Luc and Eric left Rachel's office, she and I moved to her desk. Sitting, I asked, "So . . . why did you get into leadership in the first place?"

Rachel straightened her suit slowly. "Did I ever tell you about my dad?" she asked.

I shook my head.

"He owned a fabric and tailor business in Philadelphia. And he loved what he got to do," Rachel said. "Each morning – it had to be around four thirty a.m. – I'd hear him and my mom in the kitchen. She was always fussing with his coffee and packing his lunch, and he was always talking, talking, talking." Rachel smiled. "He was excited to get to his shop.

"After school, when my friends would go and play, I'd run down to dad's shop. I always wanted to be there."

I interrupted. "Why?"

"It was the smell of the place. And I'm not talking about the fabric. I'm talking about the experience – you could smell and feel the greatness. It was so thick it drew you in. You wanted to be a part of it," Rachel said. "Dad had six employees – his 'crew,' as he liked to call them. And I swear, I knew everything about them – and they knew everything about me. I'd come in and they'd beam with delight. They were always so happy I'd arrived. They always made me feel as though I was important."

She stopped and after a pause added, "It was more than that, though: They also made me feel as though I was destined to do something important." She nodded. "They always asked me questions about my life and seemed amazed by me. For a kid, that was a special feeling.

"They were all so happy together. Laughing, talking – and my dad, he was like a conductor of a great orchestra . . . always running here and there, helping people with their music." She paused. "I loved being in that shop with my dad so much I didn't want to be anywhere else in the world.

"One day, it must have been when I was about fifteen, something happened that has stayed with me. Dad had put me to work on a gentleman's coat before going out to run some errands. And instead of sewing, I sat there watching dad's crew. I still have yet to see a team move so in sync with one another. Effortlessly, and with a natural enthusiasm, they worked through piles of garments." Rachel shook her head and said, "I'd always seen them as my heroes. They were always perfect to me. But this time . . . this time I looked closely at them. And it was as if I were looking at them for the first time: Their skin was wrinkled. Their hair was gray. Their fingers were worn, callused, and cut. They didn't even speak with the grammar I was learning in school."

Rachel lifted her head so her eyes met mine. "These were just ordinary people," she said.

"What sort of difference did that awareness make for you?" I asked.

"Let me tell you," Rachel said. "Just about then a customer came in the shop and – oh! Was he angry!" Rachel waved her hands. "Apparently, he'd gotten someone else's pants, and obviously his day was ruined. Well, do you know what happened?"

I shook my head. "What?"

"That angry man was treated like he was a hero. And ten minutes later he walked out of the shop laughing, carrying on with one of the crew, as happy as could be."

"Why was that such an important moment for you?" I asked.

Rachel smiled at me. "The crew told me after the man left that he'd really had his own pants all along. He'd simply gained too much weight to recognize his own trousers."

We laughed, and as we did, I watched a part of Rachel emerge that I hadn't seen before.

"The way they helped that man that day – it invited me to a new world," Rachel said, leaning forward. "My dad's shop was the finest in town. The mayor, the city council, visiting dignitaries – they were all regular customers. But that man, as far as the town was concerned, he was nobody. But to my dad's crew? He was a hero. They may not have known him, but he was as important to them as royalty."

Rachel took a deep breath and said, "That's when I got it. My dad treated his crew like heroes . . . so they treated each other like heroes . . . which meant that every person coming through the door was a hero."

"It sounds like your dad served the city of Philadelphia with a lot more than fabric and tailored goods," I said.

"That's for sure. And people would come from all over, oftentimes without any fabric needs at all," Rachel said. "They needed something else."

I nodded. "It also seems your dad understood the Degrees of Strength technique long before there was a name for it," I said.

"I know for a fact he did," Rachel answered. "The proof came every night when we'd walk home for supper. Just as we got to our block, he'd put his arm around me and say, 'Remember, Rachel, good is everywhere. Once you see it – you can act on it.'"

I wrote her father's words in my notebook, and Rachel sat back and crossed her arms. "So that's why I got into leadership. Ever since those days in my dad's shop, I've always wanted to create what my dad had done," she said. "For a while, I lost my way. I remember just a few years ago I started doubting the memories I just shared with you. 'You can do what my dad did *if* you have a small team or people are relying on you for employment,' I rationalized."

The room was quiet. Rachel's ability to question her own thoughts, to not believe what she was thinking, was profound. It's something I want to get better at myself.

"At that point in my leadership development, it appeared I had to choose: deliver dollars to the bottom line . . . or be the servant leader my dad was," Rachel said. "That was all turned upside down when I changed my paradigm by seeing things in Degrees of Strength. I quickly learned that the choice I thought I had to make – wasn't the choice at all! I can do both. I can be passionate and do everything under my power to make sure our company wins. And now, leadership can be about what my dad taught me, too." She took a deep breath. "In fact, if I'm going to truly help this company win, I *have* to lead like my dad did."

"There are a lot of people who want to become better servant leaders," I said. "Your dad is a good role model for us all."

Rachel smiled. "He'd appreciate hearing that."

A quiet buzzing interrupted us, and Rachel glanced at her phone. I looked at my watch. "It's about that time," I said to Rachel as she looked up. I tapped my notepad. "It's been a productive day. I've got enough here for a book."

Rachel put her hand up and gestured for me to stay in my seat. "Give me one more moment," she said. "I think you guys missed an application for Degrees of Strength that you might want to consider in the future."

I opened my notepad, grinned at her, and said, "I'm ready."

Rachel sat up and spoke with a new energy. "I've been thinking about servant leadership. When you think about it, it's easy to serve those people I agree with, have shared values with, or like," she said. "But what about those I'm not aligned with? What about people I don't like?

"I have such a passion to serve others, yet deep down I've struggled with this reality: I have discriminated in my service to others. It's been difficult to team with those I don't respect, or people who have a negative mindset, or those who are ceaseless in their plotting, positioning, or politicking.

"It's different now. With Degrees of Strength, I'm starting to interact with such people differently."

"Give me an example," I said.

Rachel looked at the ceiling for a moment. "Take Christine, for example. As a global executive she's a peer of mine," Rachel said and then laughed. "The woman can drive me crazy! She knows we need to collaborate and move fast, yet she's so analytical – plus she's compelled to challenge and question every idea and action we take." She shook her head. "And heavens, if you ever dispute something she's doing! It feels like you are being swallowed by this huge avalanche of negativity.

"In the past, I couldn't help it: I'd focus on the degrees of weakness, the degrees of qualities I despise in Christine. And it drove a wedge between us."

Rachel exhaled slowly. "But if you truly embrace the idea of servant leadership, that means I shouldn't qualify who I serve and who I don't. So, it was important for me to be accountable to myself. And, if I'm going to be responsible to the organization, it means I have to step up and serve Christine as well."

"That's not easy for many people," I said. "How do you do that?"

"Simple," Rachel said. "Well, simple in theory, but in actions it requires regular practice. And trust me. I still have a long way to go." She put her hand up and began counting with her fingers. "When I have the awareness,

1. I leverage the 3 Mind Factors by identifying and focusing on the Degrees of Strength in those characteristics in Christine that I deem crucial to our success. For example, Christine's hypersensitivity to

the details is a function of how much she cares about our success. She wants the same thing I do: for this organization to win.

2. "Then, because I'm focusing on those Degrees of Strength, my tone and words sound different when I'm with Christine – or when I'm discussing her actions with others. I'm no longer her adversary. Without even verbalizing it, I'm communicating to her that I am a partner."

"That's strong," I said. "And if you embrace the idea of servant leadership, how do you act upon the mindset shift you've made?"

Rachel held up her fingers again and continued the count.

3. "That's number three," she said. "Because I see Christine as a teammate and believe she wants the best for our organization, I am more comfortable in my communications with her. Now I can inform her of what's important and why from my perspective and ask Forward Focus Questions."

Rachel knew I was going to ask what the questions sounded like, so she held up her other hand to stop me. "They're specific, inclusive, and focused on moving us, our partnership, and our performance forward," she said. "For example,

- 'Christine, it's important to us that we move as efficiently as we can so objectives are met. What are a couple of things our collective teams can do to partner more effectively and drive greater efficiencies?'
- "Or, I could ask, 'In what ways do you want to be included earlier in processes so we can move even faster?'

- "And, after developing trust with Christine through several Degrees of Strength conversations, I may discover that she'll become more open-minded. When this happens, I can state, 'Christine, there's a perspective that your analysis and attention to details affects our ability to move fast. Yet I'm confident your reasons for taking the steps you do are to add as much value as possible. It is important that we accelerate our ability to deliver projects so we can meet obligations. What are your thoughts on this, and what ideas do you have on what we can do to become more efficient?'"

Rachel paused, as if she were looking for the right words. It didn't take her long. "This is something we talk a lot about as a team. Using the Degrees of Strength approach is not about being nice; it's about being professional. It's not about seeing things through the proverbial rose-colored glasses; it's about moving things forward. It's not just knowing people have greatness in them; it's acting upon it for improved performance. And, heaven forbid, Degrees of Strength is not about lowering expectations; it's about how to achieve our objectives faster. Roberto, Andrea, and the others, they know this – and have seen it in action.

"Since our time in the original session with you, we've terminated two team members. It wasn't easy. After reassigning them and providing coaching, they moved the needle forward. But in the end, they didn't move far enough up the scale and their performance wasn't where it needed to be. So we had to part ways."

Having visited with both Roberto and Andrea, I was aware of the dynamic of conflict between them. Now was my opportunity to ask Rachel about it. "There may be some of your team members who would like to see a couple more people let go. What are your thoughts about that?" I asked.

Rachel chuckled lightly. "I remember once as a child when I got in a fight with my brother, and my mother told me, 'You don't get to pick your blood-family. Learn to live with him, Rachel.'" She laughed again. "Well, if I chose to see everyone on our team in degrees of weakness, at some point I'd find reasons to fire all of them. But where would that get us? There are important reasons why we are set with the team we have. So, there's no waiting around, waiting to see if we can vote someone off the island. Right now, it's our responsibility to use the tools we've been given to make it all work – and win together."

I wondered if Rachel had brought this to her team's attention and explored the importance of that vision through questions. That conversation, however, would have to wait. There was something more pressing I wanted to ask her. "How does this relate to your work with Christine?"

Rachel lowered her voice slightly and said, "Confidentially, I can't figure out why this organization keeps Christine around. But that's not my decision. Right now, she's on the team. All I can do is increase the capabilities of our division in order to address difficult situations – and people – more effectively. And keep using the Degrees of Strength technique with Christine."

I reclined in my chair and reflected on how far Rachel had come. Then, something occurred to me. "What happens if you use the messages and Forward Focus Questions you gave examples of – and Christine gets defensive and never changes. What then?" I asked.

"What *then* – is where we are *now*," Rachel answered. "If our team adopts the idea that our ability to deliver our best efforts is contingent upon how other departments lead and act, then we're in a lot of trouble. Having a technique like Degrees of Strength doesn't mean life becomes perfect and you get to work in a utopian workplace. It means you regain control of your ability to effect change.

"Christine hasn't changed – yet. And she may never change. But this isn't about trying to change Christine. This is about controlling what I can control and being responsible regardless of what other people do or don't do. Once I recalibrate how I see Christine, it gives me a significant energy shift. I'm no longer wasting energy on all the things I don't like about Christine, and I'm free to use that force to develop momentum forward in other areas."

I looked at Rachel and sensed she had more to say. "What are you smiling about?" I asked.

"It's good to discuss this. It helps me take one more step forward in my journey to more fully contribute to my family and this organization," she said, and then feigned a look of mock surprise. "The truth is, I may walk out my door, see Christine – and run the opposite direction!" Then Rachel's face relaxed and she added, "But with each conversation I'm able to see my own Degrees of Strength a bit more, so I can recover quicker and get back to leading in the way I want to lead.

"Increasingly, my ability to serve others is no longer conditional upon how others serve me. Christine and I don't approach our work the same way, but no longer does that mean I have to stop supporting her or setting her up for success. Seeing her in Degrees of Strength enables me to be autonomous of her behavior – and lead from our values.

"And, like my dad said, the good is everywhere.
Once I see it, I can act on it."

CHAPTER TEN

The Five Choices Accelerators Make

Rachel's story is not over. (Is yours?) Like so many
Accelerators, Rachel doesn't approach her career as if it has a destination. It's not about getting to a certain rank of income; it's not about obtaining a certificate or level of distinction. Instead, Rachel is here to enrich the world. She's here to discover her own greatness by ensuring those around her deliver theirs. Her standing in the company will be a result of how effectively she masters this.

What any of us chooses to see, as Rachel's father coached her, is the beginning of our reality – the reality we then have to lead through. When an event occurs, a person who sees the world in degrees of weakness assesses the data and focuses on what is provable and counterproductive. "We're bad in this area and here's the evidence to prove it," this person says. This sustained approach corrodes confidence and breaks teamwork as people begin to blame each other. And performance plummets.

Conversely, when the same event occurs in the Accelerator's world, he or she assesses the data and focuses on what is provable *and useful.* Accelerators do not deny that what is provable and 'bad' exists; they simply choose not to waste time. They move to resolution faster by focusing on and leveraging the Degrees of Strength that are inherent in every situation.

It's worth asking your team: Are we spending our time talking about what is simply provable? Or are we using our resources to address what's provable *and* useful in getting us where we need to go?

For example, one person may say, "Our team is not making progress." Another person may say, "Our team is making progress." Who is telling the truth? With the 3 Mind Factors, especially #3, *we go in the direction of our focus*, Accelerators understand that both people are right. There is evidence to support both claims. However, there is something more important than debating whether or not the team is making progress, and it is the fact that both people have something in common: Together they want the team to improve.

This is where the interpretation of reality makes or breaks future performance. Which interpretation of reality will allow us to accelerate change faster, more effectively, and in a sustained way? The degrees of weakness interpretation, "our team is not making progress," shrinks confidence and gives people no foundation from which to stand and deliver. The other construct, "our team is making progress," provides evidence to participants that they can indeed succeed and gives them a ready-made base they can build upon to then improve the team's performance.

When a person understands the significance of this choice in the two approaches, transformation happens. Suddenly, there is no lack. In that moment we open our leadership, our lives, our teams, our families, and our world to new possibilities. Suddenly, we can deliver anything.

This creates an experience Accelerators crave and relentlessly pursue in every moment: the richness found in the experience of excellence. This is generated by the Degrees of Strength technique: Rather than waiting to have the experience of success – Accelerators choose to focus on the degrees to which they are already successful. Because they go in the direction of their focus, this builds their capability to succeed sooner and more often.

Ask your team (and ask your family), "Given the challenges we face, what technique to resolving these issues will give us the richer experience and accelerate us to resolution?" Then, enjoy what is delivered next.

Rachel, the members of her team, and the leaders in the previous case studies differentiate themselves because they are capable of accelerating greatness. They are Accelerators because they quickly move themselves and those around them from the current state to realizing the brilliant potential inherent in every person and situation. Ultimately, the traits of Accelerators can be summarized by the choices they make in the interactions that fill a day.

Here are the five choices Accelerators make:

1. Accelerators choose to see people, events, and situations in Degrees of Strength.
2. Accelerators choose to act with the wisdom that people already have greatness within them.
3. Accelerators choose to see what's possible – and be inspired.
4. Accelerators choose to develop people, partnerships, and performance in every interaction of every day.
5. Accelerators know that what they experience is their choice. They choose the richer experience.

Start your own Degrees of Strength case study by answering questions like these with your team and family: Where are we already making these choices? Why are these virtues important for us to expand and further develop in our work? What is our plan to do more of this?

Of course, evidence already exists that you, and those around you, are making these choices. You are already accelerating greatness and enriching the world. As you accelerate the ability in others to make these choices, you will alter the future – and accelerate all of us to the greatness that's possible.

Epilogue: Moving Forward is Never Over

I couldn't wait to get home. The experience with Rachel and her team left me inspired and even more committed to becoming a better leader, husband, and father. Isn't it remarkable, I thought, that when we use the Degrees of Strength technique, we touch those around us in remarkable ways. Just by spending time with the leaders of this organization *I had become a better person.* What will it be like when more workplaces enrich the lives of their employees in such a way?

Rachel and her team were on track to greater success. I would visit them again, but I had already seen the pattern hundreds of times and was confident they would achieve incredible things. Here's why: They were seeing their progress in this change effort in Degrees of Strength. Rather than succumb to the temptation of focusing on what they were doing wrong, who was making mistakes, and where they were stalled . . . they had learned the continuous improvement skills of learning from their experiences, authentically celebrating their progress, and staying focused on what is possible.

Unquestionably, Rachel's team would become a model for others.

I was about to leave the building when I heard Eric, whom I'd met with Luc in Rachel's office, call my name. Turning, I saw him moving quickly toward me. "Can I walk you to your car?" he asked.

"It'd be a pleasure," I said. "What's on your mind?"

"That conversation today – you should probably be aware of some things that weren't said," Eric said.

I stopped and looked at him. "Where do you want to start?"

"Rachel sees us in such Degrees of Strength that she calls us to a higher level. What I think may be possible some day in the future, she sees the evidence of where that vision is already taking place. Because she focuses there and reinforces that, it becomes a greater reality. Some days, I'm surprised by who I am becoming."

"In what ways has that made a difference for you?" I asked.

"If you go back six months, as we were being introduced to the Degrees of Strength technique, our business was in real trouble. I have to tell you, I wasn't buying this Degrees of Strength thing. As far as I was concerned it was a big distraction. I have an engineering mind. I was looking for a leadership solution that was numbers driven, a formulaic approach to move our results forward.

"When they told me, 'You can't have less than zero of any quality or strength,' they thought they were persuading me with some scientific rationale. But in my head, I was going a different direction. 'Sure,' I thought. 'So you can't have less than zero. This also means that you can't have less than zero of hatred, too. It means you have degrees of dishonesty and other undesirable traits.'

"At that time Rachel had been here for nearly a year, and I received a message from her boss. It was clear her boss wasn't happy and was looking for some heads to roll. Honestly, I was ready to 'throw her under the bus,' as they say.

"But something happened. Before I could return their call a tragedy occurred. My neighbor's child, a beautiful seven-year-old girl, died in a boating accident. My wife and I were hurt to the core. We loved that child and could not imagine for one moment the pain her parents were going through.

"A few days later we went to the funeral, and that's where I saw it. While I was expecting sadness and terrible grief, here was a room filled with celebration. There were balloons and music makers, there was laughter mixed with tears. Then, my friend stood in front of everyone and shared how badly he hurt and how he would miss his daughter and how it would be important for people to grieve on their own schedule. But for now, he wanted to celebrate the seven glorious years he knew his 'little angel here on earth.' Then his wife joined him and they asked us all a question: What was our favorite memory of this incredible child? You should have heard the stories! They were personal and funny and a remarkable testament to how this young person had enriched so many lives.

"There wasn't a dry eye in the place. But the tears were different. I'd never felt like that before." He exhaled slowly. "We were sad, but it was a sadness that revealed how much we cared, how much we loved that child. It truly was a celebration.

"On my way home, as we reflected on the event, this is when it occurred to me: This was *proof*. My friend had mastered his perspective and focus and in so doing, had found the degrees of love, the degrees of gratitude that still existed . . . even in the midst of this ugly tragedy."

Eric looked into my eyes. "I had never questioned my way of thinking – or looked at myself – like I did in that moment. Who am I to rationalize my poor behaviors? Who am I to think that my circumstances are so bad that I am entitled to be destructive with my words and actions? If my friends can see the loss of their *daughter* in Degrees of Strength, who am I to forfeit happiness and progress because things aren't going my way with comparatively smaller issues?

"When I got home, I was caught off guard by an opportunity that presented itself, one that I had been blind to before. My five-year-old boy – he had a speech challenge." Eric paused and took a breath. "He stuttered.

"We've been taking him to a speech specialist for years, with little progress. We recently went to a different doctor. After the initial examination, this woman told us, 'I think your son is perfectly fine. My guess is that your home is just a bit chaotic and fast paced. This can be overwhelming for your son. You may want to slow things down around him. Let his words catch up to his thoughts.'

"At first I was confused – and even angry. *My* home is chaotic? But then another emotion came rushing in that I hadn't felt since my son was two or three: *I think your son is perfectly fine.* My son –" Eric's voice broke. "My son is *perfectly fine* just the way he is."

Eric reached out and grabbed my arm. "I can get so much better as a dad. I've cheated my son. I've been functioning as though my son were broken, as if he had less than zero of wonderful qualities.

"In that instant, the weight – the fear – was gone. When I got home, I hugged my boy and I laughed with him. I didn't care about the stuttering anymore. All I focused on was the joy he was creating. Then, every time he wanted to speak, I stopped everything, got on my knee and smiled at him and said, 'What do you have to say to the world, Son?'

"He talked," Eric said, with a small smile growing larger. "And he talked. And the more I listened the more he talked.

"The remarkable thing is I can't remember when it happened, because – I realize now – I quit looking for it. But my boy now speaks without a stutter."

I nodded and smiled and we were silent. Finally, I said, "Congratulations, Eric. That's some of the most important leadership work you'll do in your entire life."

We started walking again when Eric said, "This experience with my neighbor and with my son made me realize something: Yes, I can argue that we can have degrees of anything – hatred, malice, jealousy. But those aren't virtues. Those aren't qualities that will move me or any of us forward. So why would I want to measure them?

"Besides, when I measure those qualities *I* suffer. I corrupt my own experience. That's when it occurred to me: Maybe I'm making leadership – *life* – way more difficult than it needs to be.

"What Rachel is giving us is a mechanism to move forward faster. She wants us to have a method to become better people . . . so we can become better leaders.

"I started using Degrees of Strength in every interaction of every day. Just like the experience with my son, it changed everything." He poked his thumb over his shoulder. "Luc? He and I used to spit venom at each other. Now, I can truly say his success is as important to me as my own.

"When I finally returned the call to Rachel's boss, I told him, 'I'll talk to you about Rachel's leadership, but only in Degrees of Strength.' He didn't know what that meant, of course. But I didn't care. I just told him about what Rachel was doing effectively as a leader, and instead of bashing her, I took responsibility and communicated where she and all of us were improving.

"Most importantly, my message was clear: I believe in Rachel."

We stopped next to my car. "Thank you, Eric," I said as we shook hands. "Eric. One more question. Why was it so important for you to run all the way out here to tell me this?"

"I figured I owed it to Rachel," he said. And then he added, "Actually, I owed it to myself."

"You are not here merely to make a living. You are here in order to enable the world to live more amply, with greater vision, with a finer spirit of hope and achievement. You are here to enrich the world, and you impoverish yourself if you forget the errand."

- WOODROW WILSON

WITH GRATITUDE

The movement of evolving how we collectively think about work is accelerating. The vision of accelerating greatness in every interaction of every day is an increasing reality. And, as implied by the word, any movement is a cooperative effort. The number of people who have had their lives improved by the Degrees of Strength technique is in the hundreds of thousands. Of this community, there are a select few leaders who provided remarkable assistance in getting this material in front of you. To list them all here would be impossible. You know who you are, however, and we sincerely thank you for the difference you're making in the world. It's an honor to be partnered with you in your effort to help others discover their greatest expression of leadership.

Our global team deserves a special acknowledgement: Each of you shows up "all in" and "every day inspired." Consequently, you inspire us in significant ways. Together, you are making a remarkable difference. Thank you for sharing your wisdom with us and the world.

And an important tip of the hat to our editor, Drew Ross, is necessary: This book achieved its height because of your keen eye and ability to challenge our thoughts and words by regularly using the Degrees of Strength technique.

Most importantly, with deep love, appreciation, and gratitude, we thank our respective families. It is largely because of you that we continue to discover our own expression of greatness.

We'd also like to acknowledge some of the thought leaders and authors who have influenced our thinking, writing, and service. It's been said that no idea is original. The application of each idea, however, evolves. Those readers who are on a quest similar to ours will have found themes and thoughts in this book that are consistent within this movement. The community is too large to list below; regardless, these thought leaders are all giants in our minds. A more comprehensive and growing list is on our website at verusglobal.com.

Who We're Inspired By

Robert Greenleaf – for his important work on servant leadership.

Douglas Reeves – his numerous books and thinking on leadership set a standard for many.

Daniel Goleman – *Emotional Intelligence* and *Primal Leadership* are both pillars.

Seth Godin – *Linchpin*, among other books, shifts paradigms and inspires.

Patricia Fripp – The world's greatest speaking coach – who has forever influenced how we communicate.

Peter Senge – His ideas in *The Fifth Discipline* are rich.

Ed Oakley and **Doug Krug** – *Enlightened Leadership* provided an important foundation.

Peter Drucker – His thoughts and work shape many conversations.

Randy Ferguson – The work with the LCA Project provides insights and wisdom that are gifts to many.

Sumantra Ghoshal – Thank you for "The Smell of the Place."

Jim Collins – *Good to Great* and *How the Mighty Fall* are favorites and provide the research confirming what our hearts are telling us.

Jeanne Purdy – College professors never retire; your lessons continue to grow in their significance and value.

RESOURCES

For valuable support to integrate and sustain the Degrees of Strength technique in your daily life – including chapter summaries and tool guides – visit **verusglobal.com** or scan the code below.

info@verusglobal.com | +1.303.577.0075
(if you prefer communicating with a real person)

After you've enjoyed this book,
please give it to another leader.

3 Mind Factors (page 26+)

1) You can only focus on one thought at a time.

2) You can't avoid a "don't."

3) You go in the direction of your focus.

Discussion Points to Apply the 3 Mind Factors:

1. What focus do we demonstrate that supports our effort to accelerate performance?

2. What approaches to our leadership are we using that reinforce a productive focus?

3. In what areas of our leadership can we increase and sustain a more productive focus?

4. How will an increased clarity of focus support our efforts to develop enhanced responsibility within the team?

5. What steps will we take to model clearer focus in our daily interactions?

Recipe for Partnership (page 34+)

1) What's working well in this area right now?

2) What created those successes?

3) What are our objectives?

4) Why are accomplishing those objectives important?

5) What can we do more of, in addition to, or better to achieve our objectives?"

Discussion Points to Apply the Recipe for Partnership:

1. In what areas of our business do we need increased alignment and shared vision?
2. What needs to be stated as important to accomplish – and why – prior to using this tool?
3. Where are there two or more groups within the organization that could benefit from a more collaborative approach?
4. When we've accomplished Steps 1-5 (above), would it be beneficial to discuss "lessons learned" in past and similar situations?
5. As action steps are identified in Step 5 (above), what questions will we ask to established shared understanding of what accountability looks like moving forward?

Trust-Based Partnerships (page 68+)

1) Demonstrate the mindset that the customer's current system or approach needs development – but the customer isn't broken.

2) Understand and build upon what's already working, thereby saving resources and building a sense of forward momentum early.

3) Ask for and utilize the customer's ideas, thus leveraging the inherent wisdom already in place.

4) Provide ample focus on and give feedback that provides clarity of the performance that's needed for success.

5) Add to momentum along the way by celebrating the small victories, thereby generating more confidence and momentum throughout the project.

Discussion Points to Apply the Trust-Based Partnerships Framework:

1. Where in the past have we succeeded in generating trust-based partnerships?
2. What steps did we take to create such partnerships?
3. In which partnerships do we want to develop greater trust?
4. Considering the partnerships we identified in question 3, why is it important that we act now to develop greater trust?
5. What steps of the Trust-Based Partnerships Framework do we want to focus on developing?

Five Choices Accelerators Make (page 109+)

1) Accelerators choose to see people, events, and situations in Degrees of Strength.

2) Accelerators choose to act with the wisdom that people already have greatness within them.

3) Accelerators choose to see what's possible – and be inspired

4) Accelerators choose to develop people, partnerships, and performance in every interaction of every day.

5) Accelerators know that what they experience is their choice. They choose the richer experience.

Discussion Points to Apply the Five Choices:

1. Where are we/am I currently making these choices successfully?
2. What steps are we/am I taking to make successful choices?
3. In what situations can we/I specifically improve in making one or more of these five choices?
4. Why is it important for us/me to improve in these choices?
5. What is our/my plan to make these choices more consistently and effectively?

NOTES FROM YOUR OWN CASE STUDY

NOTES FROM YOUR OWN CASE STUDY